1 Minute
Walk to Work

1 Minute Walk to Work

Weekly Walks to Your Greatest Year Ever

JOE SANFELIPPO

This publication is available at discount pricing when purchased in quantity for educational purposes, promotions, or fundraisers. For inquiries and details, contact the publisher at: www.jsanfelippo.com

Published by Joseph M Sanfelippo LLC

Cover Design: Joe Sanfelippo

Content Curated by: Aidan Sanfelippo

1 Minute Walk to Work by Joe Sanfelippo. —1st ed.
Paperback ISBN 979-8-218-43856-2

Praise for *1 Minute Walk to Work*

1 Minute Walk to Work: Weekly Walks to Your Greatest Year Ever exemplifies outstanding leadership in action. Joe skillfully blends humor, humility, and practicality to present a myriad of strategies for elevating your leadership capabilities. What truly sets this book apart is its genuine approach and practical insights that can be readily implemented, regardless of your experience level or current leadership role. It's a transformative guide that empowers readers to achieve their best year yet.

Beth Houf
Principal, Author, Speaker, National Principal of the Year

If you are looking for a book that will make you reflect and push you to act, then 1 Minute Walk to Work by Joe Sanfelippo is a must-read! Filled with practical wisdom from his brief walks to work over the last few years, Joe's words will inspire you to walk with purpose and more importantly, lead with purpose.

Jimmy Casas
Leadership Coach, Educator, Author, Speaker

For years, I looked forward to Joe Sanfelippo's 1 Minute Walk to Work videos; they always made me not only smile, but also think. Ultimately, they helped make me a better leader. Now, many of these "walks" are compiled in this wonderful book. Reading Joe's reflections on how we get better at the important art of leadership is an easy way for readers to consider the actions we take, the words we speak, and the mindsets we must adopt to fulfill not only our own potential, but also the potential of the students and staff we serve. These short, powerful leadership nuggets are organized in a way that allows readers to study leadership challenges that typically occur throughout a school year and reflect on how we can best meet these challenges to help us and those we lead perform at our highest levels. I highly recommend this excellent book!

Dr. Jeffrey Zoul
Author of Improving Your School One Week at a Time

This book is a treasure trove of leadership wisdom, conveyed simply, but at the highest of levels, of what it looks like to lead effectively throughout the school year. Each walk provides practical, impactful lessons delivered in a way that leaders can't help but feel as if Dr. Sanfelippo was talking just to them. The reflections and activities are designed to foster growth and build leadership capacity, ensuring that leaders feel supported rather than judged. Whether you read this as a team or are a leader trying to take better care of your people, this book is an invaluable resource for those looking to elevate their leadership practice.

Amber Teamann
Executive Director of Tech and Innovation, Crandall ISD

Whether you are leading a classroom, leading a building, or leading at the district level, Joe Sanfelippo has created an invaluable resource that will support educators through every phase of the school year. The text, which is elevated with the inclusion of the accompanying videos, covers a spectrum of topics that will help educators tackle a number of challenges while also sparking ideas for how to enhance existing practices within the organization. Whether struggling to address a logistical issue or looking for ways to contribute to a positive culture, Joe has a video, tip, or suggestion for everyone. The thing that makes this book even more special is Joe - his enthusiasm and zeal are truly infectious and inspirational. I cannot wait to share this book with colleagues!

Dr. Tony Sinanis
Superintendent, Author, NY State Principal of the Year

Actionable inspiration. There are not many people who can make you think, feel, and smile in 60 seconds or less. But Joe Sanfelippo is one of them. And he's crafted something educators actually need in the pages that follow. 1 Minute Walk to Work is more than a book — it's a mindset that will elevate who you want to be.

Dr. Brad Gustafson
Principal, Author, and Optimistic Fan of the
Minnesota Vikings

America's favorite Superintendent shares an inspiring work to support every student, throughout every season, of every educator's school year. Sanfelippo's latest, 1 Minute Walk to Work, will motivate, educate, and invigorate. A must read.

Weston Kieschnick
Author, Speaker

Joe Sanfelippo has mesmerized educators over the years with practical advice during his walks to work. By combining wit and targeted messages using video, he has motivated countless people looking to grow their practice. This book combines the best of both worlds as Joe weaves additional context to each video to inspire all educators to reflect on their work and make an even greater impact in the field of education.

Eric Sheninger
Best-selling Author and Keynote Speaker

Joe Sanfelippo shares a refreshing and motivating read that encourages leaders and professionals to shift their mindset, embrace their roles with enthusiasm, and inspire others to do the same. The book's practical advice and personal stories make it a valuable resource for anyone seeking to enhance their leadership skills and job satisfaction. As an individual that has personally followed all of the Walks, each and every one is a positive shot in the arm that makes you think and pushes you to be a better person. 1 Minute Walk to Work provides an insightful look at how small, consistent efforts can lead to significant changes.

Ben Gilpin
Superintendent

Joe's latest book is a heartfelt guide for leaders navigating the complexities of their work. He skillfully addresses the gap between our initial aspirations and the challenging realities of leadership. Throughout the book, Joe fearlessly dives into the questions, doubts, and fears that resonate with those of us in leadership positions, offering practical and empowering strategies to overcome them.

From the hopeful anticipation of a new year to the reflective moments at its conclusion, Joe authentically captures the emotional journey of leadership. His wisdom and encouragement will empower you to not just survive, but thrive in your leadership journey, making this year your most impactful yet.

Jessica Cabeen
Principal of Alternative Programs, Author, Speaker, MN
Principal of the Year

If you've listened to or watched Joe's 1 Minute Walk to Work videos over the years, you can hear his voice clearly as you read these pages. Joe provides a blueprint for leaders to connect with the people they serve by creating community, common behaviors, conversations that create stories, and celebrations of the small moments that foster positive experiences. Any leading willing to implement the weekly strategies will have the greatest year ever.

Dwight Carter
Director of Student Support Systems, Author, Speaker

In one of the most inspirational education books to date, Sanfelippo combines motivational insights with practical strategies to focus on what matters most - our people. In 1 Minute Walk to Work, you'll discover insightful video reflections, thought-provoking questions, and activities designed to foster meaningful conversations and personal growth. Regardless of your role in education, this book is an invaluable resource for leading with purpose, building human capacity, and making a lasting impact on your community while building the greatest year ever.

Thomas C. Murray
Director of Innovation, Future Ready Schools,
Washington, D.C.

The *1 Minute Walk To Work* is full of engaging and empowering reminders to focus on what we control. The combination of text and videos serves as a "coach on your shoulder" and "guide on your side" as we navigate the blessed burden of leadership. In an age that can sometimes feel like information overload, Sanfelippo messages are simple and significant!

Ken Williams, Coach, Author, Speaker - Unfold The Soul

Dedication

This book is for anyone who finds purpose in helping others smile, and laugh, and think, and feel, because when you chase smiles, you tend to find your own.

Table of Contents

Introduction

Homecoming in small towns across the country is amazing, and it's no different in Fall Creek, Wisconsin, home of the Fall Creek Crickets. The PreK-12 building sits in the middle of town and is where most things happen in Fall Creek. The village of 1,300 people is completely connected to its school, as evidenced by the number of community members who came out to watch the homecoming parade filled with high school athletes and clubs on this particular day. The leaves in Wisconsin were changing; there was a crisp, cool breeze, and the streets were lined with villagers waiting to wave at the high school students who were loaded up on overflowing flatbeds and trucks to the point that they needed to walk alongside the vehicle. As the parade made its way through the village, they turned the corner to the elementary school where all 325 Kindergarten through 5th-grade students were outside sitting on the curb waiting in anticipation for the high school kids, donned in their home jerseys, to walk past, hoping to get a smile or a wave. As they approached, the high school athletes who walked along the side of the trucks made their way to the elementary students like moths drawn to a flame. Smiles and waves turned into high fives and hugs. The volleyball team was first. Then, the cross-country team turned the corner with the same result. Finally, the football team made their way to the elementary group with the same result. The look of excitement and joy on the faces of the kids was only matched by the teachers who stood behind them. The kids in the parade were theirs…the kids they had taught years prior. The kids were older, but the smiles remained, and now they were giving those smiles to a new batch of Crickets who will never forget the connection with a real person, not just a number on a field or court that they watch on a Friday night. I got home on the night of the parade, already beaming with pride for our school, and saw a picture on Facebook of the high school kids high-fiving all our elementary students. There were many positive comments, but one struck me more than any:

"My kindergartner came home today, and the first thing he said was, 'I got a high five from Taylor!' I don't know who you are, Taylor, but I will never be able to thank you enough for how you made my son feel."

The next morning, I woke up still thinking about the impact that kids have on kids, schools, and communities. When we moved into Fall Creek, Wisconsin, we *really* moved into Fall Creek, Wisconsin. We bought the house directly across the street from school. My walk to school is roughly one minute from door to door. It's early, and I'm loud, so to let my family sleep I walk across the street to my office to get some things done, but mostly to not wake them up. As I was getting ready to leave, I couldn't help but think about the events of the day before and how more people should know about the amazing things happening in this small town in Wisconsin. I had a phone, an idea, and about 60 seconds to get into the building. 6 years and 100 walks later, here we are. I didn't do a walk every week because I didn't have something new to talk about every week. Every walk is authentic and every walk helped me think of ways I could be better for the people I was lucky enough to lead. Many of the walks are about things I screwed up, in hopes that leaders watching would not have to go through the same issues. Mostly, it was a way to shine a light on the incredible people who have made an unbelievable difference in the lives of thousands of kids in a small town in northwest Wisconsin. People like Taylor, who impacted a kid and a family, without even knowing.

What started with a walk to shine the light on the incredible educators we have in Fall Creek, Wisconsin, turned into a process that provided purpose to how and why I lead. The stories are all real. Most of the time, they are things I wished I had known when I was going through them, but what I realized was that people found themselves in the story, and it made them smile, laugh, think, and feel. That made me want to tell more. The impact of our colleagues and the momentum a comment, tweet, call, or text had about every walk showed me the power in each story.

1 Minute Walk to Work: Weekly Walks to Your Greatest Year Ever comprises the most popular walks created throughout the last six years. The timing of the walks seemed important because of the time of year they took place. The book is divided into four leadership seasons, and the walks were typically thoughts about things going on at that point in the school year from a leadership perspective, so it made sense to keep them in that order.

Each walk in this book also comes with a QR code that sends you directly to the video of that particular walk. This was important to me because the printed pages you see are literal transcriptions of the walks, but sometimes, seeing the video gives the walk more context and makes it easier to share with colleagues if you choose. Also, anyone who doesn't typically bear the bitter cold of Wisconsin winters can smile that they don't live in a place where the wind makes their face hurt.

At the end of each walk are two reflection questions for the week to think about during that particular time of the year. Sometimes I would think about those questions, sometimes, I would journal about them, and sometimes they were questions I started out our leadership team meetings with, but all the questions helped me reflect on leading from a place where I would want to be led. A place where voices are heard, people are seen, and ideas are valued. I hope that they take you on a similar path.

Each walk also has one potential activity to do with your staff. The activity may spark a conversation and can help you start a staff meeting. The activities are not intended to be full-blown initiatives. Starting something new every week is a recipe for disaster. The activities are intended to be a catalyst for conversation and an opportunity to walk with purpose.

Whether you drive an hour to work or live across the street, there is always a time during the day when you are walking into the space in which you lead. I hope you take that time to reflect on the impact you have as a leader, the impact your words and actions have on those around you, and the impact your mindset has on the enjoyment of your job, one walk at a time. Remember: We're all in this thing together.

New Leaders:
Before We Begin

Every year there are many new superintendents and principals walking into their offices for the first time to start a brand-new career. And as I started my 11th year here, this is a good time to offer a couple of pieces of advice for new leaders as they start in their new roles. First and foremost, you don't know everything. And guess what? They know you don't know everything. So don't try to pretend to know everything. It's OK that you don't know everything. The second thing is the farther you get from the classroom, the harder it is to make suggestions about what could happen in that place. So make sure you stay connected there. The third thing is that people tell me all the time that all they want to do is hire great people and get out of the way. No, you don't. You're not a search firm. Hire great people, but then help them get better. Lastly, take the *work* seriously, but don't take *yourself* too seriously.

This job can become really isolating, lonely, and depressing unless you bring people along with you. Leadership is a good job. It's a better job when you build a team. It's the best job when the team that you build is focused on impacting others.

Self-Reflection Questions for the Leader:

Self-awareness and Continuous Learning: Reflect on areas of educational leadership where you feel least confident. How can you leverage the expertise within your team and the broader educational community to fill these gaps?

Building and Supporting Your Team: Consider the statement, "Hire great people, but then help them get better." What specific actions can you take to not only attract talented individuals but also foster their professional growth and development?

Initiate a Listening Tour:

Activity Overview: Spend your first few weeks meeting with teachers, staff, students, and parents to listen to their experiences, insights, and suggestions. This will help you understand the strengths and areas for improvement within the school community and demonstrate your commitment to inclusivity and collaboration. The most meaningful piece of the listening tour is how and when you will follow up with what you have learned. Transparency starts with closing the loop on what you learned and how it will impact you moving forward.

The Seasons: Building Throughout the Year

The rhythm of a school year, through its distinct seasons, offers challenges and opportunities for school leaders. Each season, with its unique character, demands a thoughtful approach to ensure a thriving school environment. We can think of the seasonal focus areas as follows:

Season One: Anticipation
Season Two: Momentum
Season Three: Renewal
Season Four: Culmination

Season One: Anticipation (July-August)

In the calm before the proverbial storm, leaders lay the groundwork for success. This season is characterized by strategic planning, aligning the curriculum with educational standards, and tailoring professional development to meet teachers' needs. Infrastructure, from classrooms to technology, must be reviewed and updated to support the upcoming academic demands. Engaging with the community through meetings and communications sets a positive tone, ensuring a collaborative start to the year.

This is a time for vision setting, where leaders refine the school's goals and align them with district objectives, ensuring a coherent path forward. Professional development takes center stage, with workshops and training sessions designed to equip teachers with the latest pedagogical strategies and technological tools. Facility upgrades and safety protocols are scrutinized and enhanced, guaranteeing a welcoming and secure environment for all. Community outreach affords leaders the opportunity to build partnerships and open dialogue with parents and local organizations, setting a tone for the year.

Season Two: Momentum (September-December)

As students return, the focus shifts to building momentum. This period involves establishing routines, fostering a positive school culture, and navigating the academic process necessary to complete the first semester successfully. As students fill the corridors, the focus shifts to creating a dynamic learning environment. This phase is crucial for establishing clear expectations, embedding robust routines, and fostering a culture of respect and achievement. Parental engagement is heightened through regular updates and involvement opportunities, strengthening the school-home partnership. The close of season two is the holiday break and marks a time for reflection and anticipation of the next phase.

Season Three: Renewal (January-March)

After the holidays, a sense of renewal begins. Resolutions have been started (some ended) and this often becomes a time when we can see a dip in momentum and morale. This is a critical juncture for evaluating progress toward yearly goals and making necessary adjustments. Attention to student well-being is heightened, addressing the mid-year fatigue that can impact performance. This season is also key for preparing students and staff for the upcoming assessments, with targeted support and review sessions. Community engagement continues with events and initiatives that refresh the school spirit.

The new year brings a chance to rejuvenate and refocus. This mid-year checkpoint is critical for assessing progress against academic goals and adjusting strategies as necessary. The curriculum may be revisited to ensure alignment with student needs and state standards. A renewed emphasis on student well-being helps to combat the post-holiday slump, with counseling and support services in full swing. Preparation for spring assessments begins, with mock exams and review sessions to bolster confidence and competence. Community events, such as science fairs and art shows, highlight the talents within the school, fostering pride and unity.

Season Four: Culmination (April-June)

In the home stretch, the focus intensifies on achieving academic objectives and celebrating milestones. Preparations for standardized testing, graduation ceremonies, and transitions (such as moving from middle to high school) dominate this period. It's a time for recognizing student and staff accomplishments and setting the stage for the subsequent academic year. Reflective practices are employed, gathering insights from the year's experiences to inform future planning.

As the year draws to a close, the focus sharpens on culmination and celebration. The pressure of standardized testing is met with a well-coordinated support system, easing student anxieties and maximizing performance. Graduation and transition planning become paramount, honoring achievements and preparing students for their next academic chapter. Reflection is a key theme, with staff and students alike taking stock of the year's successes and challenges. This feedback loop is crucial for continuous improvement, informing planning for the following year. Community celebrations and recognitions reinforce the collective achievement, ending the year on a note of accomplishment and anticipation for the future.

The leadership seasons all come with highs and lows. Trust from those you lead is often found in the moments that are unanticipated. When we are prepared for what we can control, those times that surprise us can be reduced. Knowing what is happening in each season and being able to create momentum in times that don't surprise us, will help get us through the times that do. Each season is unique, and the reflections allow us to be as present as possible in each one.

Anticipation

This is the calm before the proverbial storm. You may be new to the position, new to a district, or just need a revamp regarding how you want to lead. Whatever your situation, there is always a great deal of excitement around a new school year, and that has an impact on the way we operate as leaders. Season One in leadership tends to be more about adrenaline than anything else. When we run solely on adrenaline, we get caught up in the excitement and veer away from our systems and frameworks. The beginning of the school year is coming, and before long, the empty hallways of offices and schools will be filled with the incredible noises of kids and our staff.

This is an excellent time for us as leaders to start thinking about who we are as leaders and what values we hold true when it comes to leading our group. As we create value statements or a vision to help guide our actions, remember that less is more when it comes to what you want to get out as a leader. When I talk to schools about telling the story of their classroom, building, team, or district, I always come back to making sure the message is *Simple, Unique,* and *Repeatable.* Season One is an optimal time for you to develop who you are as a leader and how you will project that to those you lead in a simple, unique, and repeatable way. Knowing you as the leader and how you respond when things go well AND when they don't will invite more conversations and help show how you lead from a set of values everyone can lean into. Welcome to Season One...

LEADERSHIP CHALLENGE WEEK 1:

Give Yourself a Chance

**Alright, everybody, Saturday morning,
Fall Creek, Wisconsin, one minute walk to work,
and here's what I'm thinking about today...**

Two of our kids love track. I hate running, but I love my kids, and my kids love track. So I love track. Allie sprints. When she's out there sprinting, I'm screaming at her, "You gotta go, you gotta go."

Last year, after a race, she came up to me and said, "You know that's ridiculous, right? You don't think I know I got to run as fast as possible. It's a sprint, Daddy. It's literally all you do."

My son Kael runs middle distance, so he finds his way around the track several times, and I get to yell more stuff at him. But one thing I constantly yell at him is, "Give yourself a chance." Because I know that if he keeps it close, he's going to find a way to catch the group that's in front of him almost every time.

Last year, I asked him, "How are you able to find that extra speed at the end of all these races?" He said that with every step that got him closer, he got this jolt of adrenaline and more belief that he could catch the group in front of him. I'm thinking about that now because that's all we're trying to do. There are no guarantees. There are no magic beans. Everything that we do is trying to give ourselves the best chance. And the best chance for us often comes in the belief that what we do impacts those around us. Because when we see the impact, the belief grows.

▶▷ **So the leadership challenge for next week is simply this:**

What are you doing to give yourself the best chance? Is it how you start your day or end your day? Is it finding purpose in writing or reading or exercising or celebrating something that happened? I can't tell you what it is for you, but what I can tell you is that you are the one who gives every kid in that room the best chance just by showing up. So give yourself a chance by knowing the impact of what you do.

Just gotta take care of each other. Alright, people, that's all I've got. We're all in this thing together. Have a great week, everybody… Go Crickets!

Self-Reflection Questions for the Leader:

- How am I ensuring that I give myself the best chance each day to make a positive impact in our school?
- In what ways can I support staff members in recognizing and maximizing their potential to positively influence students?

Best Chance Routine Workshop

- Activity Overview: Host a workshop at which staff members reflect on their daily routines and identify practices that give them the best chance for a successful day. Encourage sharing of personal strategies for starting or ending the day positively and discuss how these routines impact their presence and effectiveness in the classroom.

People Over Plan

**Alright, everybody, Saturday morning,
Fall Creek, Wisconsin, one minute walk to work,
and here's what I'm thinking about today...**

Two weeks ago, we had the graduation ceremony for the class of 2020, and it was outside and the graduates could only invite two guests. So we live streamed the event, so people who were unable to attend could still see the ceremony. We were all set. Our team did a fantastic job of coordinating this event, so our seniors had one more opportunity to celebrate.

Before everyone arrived, we checked everything. We checked the live stream. We checked the staging area. We checked the microphones. We checked to make sure the kids had water. All of it. We were ready to go. Then people started showing up and things just started going sideways. The stage area needed to be adjusted. Kids needed more water. But most importantly, the live stream that we had promised everybody decided to stop working.

And I'm sitting there in the middle of the ceremony, just getting more and more frustrated. There's nothing I could do at that particular time. At the height of that frustration, a young woman named Paige stepped up to the microphone and made me forget about

16

everything. She talked about her friends and her teachers and the senior drive, where they drove through town and the community came out and just cheered at the top of their lungs for these kids.

And then she said, "Because people are amazing, and that's why I don't hate coronavirus." So after the ceremony, we fixed the livestream and got it up. So people could still see the video and it wasn't perfect, but it worked the best that we could at that particular time.

▷▷ So the leadership challenge for next week is simply this:

The only promise I can make you for the upcoming year is that parts of your plan will fail. But your people won't. For 6 minutes and 16 seconds, I got a chance to see what one person can help build: Her family, her friends, her teachers, her community. So don't ever forget why these plans are in place to begin with. It's the people. And as Paige says, "People are amazing."

Just gotta take care of each other. Alright, people, that's all I've got. We're all in this thing together. Have a great week, everybody... Go Crickets!

Self-Reflection Questions for the Leader:

- How am I ensuring that my planning and decision-making process prioritizes the needs and strengths of our people?
- In what ways can I foster a culture where the value of individuals is recognized and celebrated, even when plans fall short?

People Over Plans Discussion Circle

- Activity Overview: Organize a circle discussion for staff to share stories where things didn't go as planned but the strength and resilience of their community (students, colleagues, families) made a positive difference. Highlight the importance of focusing on people and relationships over rigid plans.

LEADERSHIP CHALLENGE WEEK 3:

New Stuff

**Alright, everybody, Saturday morning,
Fall Creek, Wisconsin, one minute walk to work,
and here's what I'm thinking about today...**

Schools across the country are back in session this week, which means you get to see a lot of these memes pop up about the first week of school. My favorite is the one that says, "There's no tired like first-day-teacher tired." This makes me laugh every time because first-day-teacher tired isn't about the first day of school; it's about the fact that these people have been in their classrooms for two weeks until all hours of the evening getting ready for the first day of school. Just running on adrenaline the whole time, and then when the kids leave after the first day, that's when the real tired sets in. A lot of times, it's because of all the new stuff we're trying to implement at the beginning of the year. The problem with that is that the new stuff is replacing the new stuff from the year before.

It's like every house that I've ever lived in has a junk drawer. Where you have something new, and then all of a sudden, after you use it for a little bit, you put it in the junk drawer because you don't really know where it's supposed to go, but you know you might need it at some point so you just put it off to the side. We do this all the time. You get the shiny new toy that replaces the shiny new toy from the year before. And then, six months after that, you realize that the shiny new toy from the year before worked, and then you want to bring it back, but it takes longer to bring it back when it never should have left to begin with.

 So, the leadership challenge for next week is simply this:

New doesn't automatically mean better. Think about two things you did last year that you're the most proud of. Make sure you have a plan in place for those two things to continue. The plan should be understood by everyone you lead and they should also have an understanding as to why those two practices will continue and what it will take to do so. Then, think about something new and how you want to implement it over time. Because I'm just going to be honest with you: 90% of the time, it's not about the stuff; it's about the person delivering the stuff that has the biggest impact on the result, and that's you.

Just gotta take care of each other. Alright, people, that's all I've got. We're all in this thing together. Have a great week, everybody...
Go Crickets!

Self-Reflection Questions for the Leader:

- How am I ensuring that I'm focusing on the effectiveness of the person and not just on new initiatives or tools?

- What can I do to balance the excitement of new things with the proven value of established practices?

Self-Care and Connection

- Activity Overview: Hold a session at which teachers can learn and practice self-care techniques and explore ways to deepen connections with colleagues and students. Include stations for mindfulness, exercise, healthy eating, and effective communication.

Getting You Ready for School

**Alright, everybody, Saturday morning,
Fall Creek, Wisconsin, one minute walk to work,
and here's what I'm thinking about today...**

In Wisconsin, we're about two weeks away from having staff come back into the building, which essentially means that they've been here for two weeks getting their room ready, and this got me thinking about when I was teaching. I used to do everything I could to make sure that the room was perfect for kids when they walked in. You know. I remember I built this space shuttle that they could read in. I had the Plinko board, and I had all the name tags perfectly placed on the desk. I got the ruler out and made sure that they were equidistant from the side. I had all the inspirational posters. I had the cat poster that hangs on the wall; it tells the kids to hang in there.

I had all of that stuff. I just wanted them to walk in with that sense of excitement that they were, you know, ready for the year. What I didn't realize was that I spent so much time with that that by the time they got to school, I was already tired, and I didn't realize it because I had been running on adrenaline for two weeks.

 ## So, the leadership challenge for next week is simply this:

Do everything that you have to do to get your room ready for the year. But don't ever forget that the most important thing to get ready in your room is you. Take care of yourself, get your sleep, connect with your colleagues, have conversations, you know, make these connections because kids are going to show up in your room, and they're going to find their name on a desk and realize that they're supposed to be in that room. Then they're going to turn to you and truly learn if they belong in that room.

Cat posters don't make kids hang in there if, when they look into our eyes, they don't think we want them to. We just have to be there for them. We have to be there for our colleagues, too. It's hard to take care of kids when we're not taking care of each other.

Just gotta take care of each other. Alright, people, that's all I've got. We're all in this thing together. Have a great week, everybody... Go Crickets!

Self-Reflection Questions for the Leader:

- How am I prioritizing my well-being and that of staff members to ensure a positive start to the school year?
- In what ways can I foster a culture of self-care and mutual support among all staff members?

Past Successes and New Ventures Mapping

- Activity Overview: Facilitate a session where staff members map out two of their proudest achievements from the past year and identify something new they want to try this year. This activity encourages a balance between leveraging proven strategies and exploring new approaches.

Get To vs. Got To

**Alright, everybody, Saturday morning,
Fall Creek, Wisconsin, one minute walk to work,
and here's what I'm thinking about today...**

few weeks ago, I saw a video circulating of Ernie Johnson from the NBA and TNT talking to Alabama's football team. And it was brilliant. He's incredible, by the way. And he was talking about the idea that he has a "get-to" job, not a "got-to" job, he *gets* to do this work. And I feel the same way. I love leading in Fall Creek, Wisconsin. I *get* to do this work. There are a lot of things to do in a get-to job. There's a lot of got-to stuff to do, even though this is a get-to job.

I'm a list person, so I write stuff down on a list and check it off as I go. There are two types of list people in the world: there are list people who write stuff down on a list and check it off as they go along, and then there are list people like me, who write stuff down on the list, and check it off as they go along. But the difference is this, if I do something that's not on the list, I'm going to write it down on the list and check it off because you should get credit for that. The problem with the list is there's not a lot of get-to stuff on that got-to list. If I'm consumed with the got-to list, I don't appreciate my get-to job.

▶▶ So, the leadership challenge for next week is simply this:

When we see our position as a get-to position, the got-to list in that get-to position makes more sense. And maybe it's that simple, or maybe it's that we need to take some of the get-to stuff and put it on the got-to list. Maybe do it a couple of times before you check it off.

Just gotta take care of each other. Alright, people, that's all I've got. We're all in this thing together. Have a great week, everybody... Go Crickets!

Self-Reflection Questions for the Leader:

- How am I framing my responsibilities as opportunities ("get to") rather than obligations ("got to")?
- What can I do to help my team reframe their "got to" tasks as "get to" opportunities?

"Get To" Reflection Session

- Activity Overview: Host a reflection session during which staff members identify aspects of their job they feel privileged to do ("get to" do) and discuss how these can transform their perspective on their daily responsibilities ("got to" do).

LEADERSHIP CHALLENGE WEEK 6:

Eat. Rest. Laugh.

Alright, everybody, Saturday morning, Fall Creek, Wisconsin, one minute walk to work, and here's what I'm thinking about today...

What tends to happen is that people who work in school spend so much time taking care of everybody else that they don't take care of themselves. They're making sure that the room is ready. They make sure that the parents get what they need. They want that moment when the kid walks into the classroom and immediately feels like they belong. I think a lot of times, we're just all running on adrenaline. Happened to me earlier this week. And when I run on adrenaline, I go, and I go, and I go.

One of the things that happens is I forget to eat. I got home at the end of the day and hadn't eaten all day. I walked into the house, and there was a package of organic peanut butter cookies on the counter. I thought, "Organic, good. Peanut butter, good. Cookie, good." So I grabbed a cookie and ate it. It wasn't good. So I thought it must be me. So I grabbed another one. I'm eating. I got halfway through the second cookie, and I said to my wife, Andrea, "These

28

cookies are not good." And she said, "You're going to want to look at the package." So I looked at the package, and it said organic peanut butter cookies with a picture of a dog in the bottom right-hand corner, which I clearly missed.

So, the leadership challenge for next week is simply this:

I'm not trying to turn this into some philosophical, motivational concept that the brand promise didn't match the brand experience or that all groups need different things. I'm just telling you, eat real food, get some rest, and laugh a little bit because it's hard to take care of other people when you're not taking care of yourself. If you're tired and you're hungry, you're going to make bad decisions. Those bad decisions come with consequences, like when your daughter continues to say to you, "Hey, Daddy, come get your treat," and then laughs hysterically, which makes it almost worth it–almost.

**Just gotta take care of each other. Alright, people, that's all I've got. We're all in this thing together. Have a great week, everybody...
Go Crickets!**

Self-Reflection Questions for the Leader:

- How am I ensuring that I maintain a balance of nutrition, rest, and humor in my life to enhance my leadership effectiveness?
- In what ways can I encourage and model self-care among the staff to improve their well-being and decision-making?

Well-being Lifestyle Challenge

- Overview: Initiate a month-long challenge encouraging staff members to adopt healthier habits, like eating real food, getting adequate rest, and incorporating laughter into their day. Provide a platform for participants to share experiences and support each other.

Build Back Relationships

**Alright, everybody, Saturday morning,
Fall Creek, Wisconsin, one minute walk to work,
and here's what I'm thinking about today...**

First time I got sent to the principal's office as a kid, I was in third grade and my principal, Mr. Bright, used to walk around school all the time, pop his head in the classrooms, say hi, that kind of thing.

I remember on this particular day, he walked into our third grade classroom. He walks in, and he says, "Good morning, everybody." And in my infinite third-grade wisdom, I decided to respond with, "Good morning, Not-so", because "not so bright" is a super funny thing to say as a third grade kid. But it wasn't super funny for Mr. Bright, nor was it funny for my mom when my mom got called. But, the interesting thing about that situation was after that incident I started avoiding the office at all costs. I used to go down different hallways, go out different doors, whatever. I just did not want to go past the office because I was embarrassed about what had happened until Mr. Bright started finding me in places and just having conversations about nothing. But he was just trying to connect. I didn't know what he was doing until I started working with kids. He was just trying to build back the relationship after tough conversations. I think we, as leaders, need to think about what that really looks like.

▶▶ So, the leadership challenge for next week is simply this:

What are we doing as leaders to build back relationships after tough conversations? You know, you must have tough conversations, but we also must figure out ways to help people move forward after them. Part of our job is to help build a bridge to get people going in the right direction. So there are times when I think that goes really well. There are other times that I had just totally failed miserably at that. I need to be better.

**Just gotta take care of each other. Alright, people, that's all I've got. We're all in this thing together. Have a great week, everybody...
Go Crickets!**

Self-Reflection Questions for the Leader:

- How might understanding the emotions and perspectives of others change the way I approach difficult conversations?
- Have you noticed staff members or students avoiding you after a tough conversation? What steps can you take to bridge the gap and initiate a positive interaction?

Relationship Repair:

- Activity Overview: Encourage staff members to share their experiences and reflections in staff meetings or through a shared digital platform, fostering a culture of open communication and mutual support.

Value and Connection

**Alright, everybody, Saturday morning,
Fall Creek, Wisconsin, one minute walk to work,
and here's what I'm thinking about today...**

Today, we take our firstborn son to college, which you might think makes me feel really old, but it doesn't. Actually, getting winded on a one-minute walk to work makes me feel more old than taking my son to college. So the last month has been filled with all these lasts for Aidan—you know, the last time we do this as a family, the last time we do that as a family.

We were up North at my in-laws' place a couple of weeks ago; it was the last time that we were all together as a family before he went to college. My in-laws have this beautiful land and they got all these little old golf carts that we kind of tool around on and that kind of thing. And my in-laws are just incredible people.

And often, at the end of the trip, everybody will jump on a golf cart and buzz around the land, and they will just kind of be there with each other. And I actually had to leave early on this particular trip, and I got a call from my wife as they were coming home, and she said, "You know, we took the golf cart ride before everybody took off," and when they got back to the house, her mom said to her, "Let's just go one more time." She didn't want it to end.

I think that whatever we go through and whenever we go through it, everyone reflects more positively on interactions when you provide value and when you provide connection.

So, the leadership challenge for next week is simply this:

As you get back into the swing of school, and you start with kids and you start with your faculty and that kind of thing, remember, it doesn't matter if you've been doing this for 1 year, 5 years, 10 years or if you've been on this ride for 15 years, 20 years, whatever.

It's going to be the only time they're in your space with you. If you provide value and connection, they'll not want it to end.

Just gotta take care of each other. Alright, people, that's all I've got. We're all in this thing together. Have a great week, everybody... Go Crickets!

Self-Reflection Questions for the Leader:

- How am I ensuring that every interaction in my school creates a sense of value and connection for those involved?
- In what ways can I improve the quality of interactions to make them more memorable and impactful?

Value and Connection Days

- Activity Overview: Initiate "Connection Days," during which the leader spends the day engaging with different classrooms and departments, focusing on understanding and addressing their unique needs and contributions.

LEADERSHIP CHALLENGE WEEK 9:

Don't Chase Flies

**Alright, everybody, Saturday morning,
Fall Creek, Wisconsin, one minute walk to work,
and here's what I'm thinking about today...**

A few weeks ago, I was sitting in a cabin in Northern Wisconsin in the early morning, just light enough that I could see everything. And the windows were open so that I could hear the birds and the wind. It is just a great space to read, write, and start your day with purpose. It's beautiful.

As I sat there enjoying everything about the space, I heard this one fly buzzing around that cabin. It would get louder, and I'd look for it. And then it would fly away. I could still hear it. Everywhere it went, I could still hear it.

It got to be so annoying because it became the only thing that I could hear, even in this beautiful spot. I'm a problem solver, so I got up. I started going after it. I started chasing this fly. So here I am in Northern Wisconsin, hunting one fly. I started to get so annoyed because I couldn't find it anywhere.

And at the peak of that aggravation, Allie walked up from downstairs, gave me a hug, and said, "Good morning, Daddy."

And then Kael came up and gave me that assurance nod. He's says, "What's up, bro?" Andrea came out. And Aidan came out. The dogs came out. And here we are: we're just with our family, just starting our day.

The funny thing for me is when they came out, I forgot that the fly was there. When they woke up and walked out, I remembered why we were there, and the buzzing of a fly–that had no understanding of why we were there–didn't matter nearly as much.

▶▶ So, the leadership challenge for next week is simply this:

There will always be people in this world who think they know what you do because they went to school. They will make judgments about you without knowing anything about you. And sometimes it's loud, and often it's annoying. But instead of chasing the fly, chase the smiles of the kids and colleagues with whom you work, because when you do that, you forget that the fly is there and you remember why you are.

Just gotta take care of each other. Alright, people, that's all I've got. We're all in this thing together. Have a great week, everybody... Go Crickets!

Self-Reflection Questions for the Leader:

- How am I focusing my attention on the positive aspects of my role, rather than getting distracted by external criticism?
- In what ways can I model resilience and positivity in the face of criticism or misunderstanding?

Smile-Chasing Team Activity

- Activity Overview: Smile Chasing Project: Encourage staff members to note and share moments that bring joy to their day. Leave post-it notes in staff lounges with a board where the notes can be displayed.

LEADERSHIP CHALLENGE WEEK 10:

What If?

**Alright, everybody, Saturday morning,
Fall Creek, Wisconsin, one minute walk to work,
and here's what I'm thinking about today...**

We sent out a survey this week that had three questions: What's going well? What are you struggling with? What's one thing that we could do here to make it a better experience for you?

For the first couple hours we got a ton of responses. I started looking at the number and I'm thinking to myself, "Aw man, this is not going to end well. But I really want to look through these right now." And I started looking through the responses and our parents were incredible. They were so respectful. And the things that they were asking for are things that we could do.

And what struck me was they didn't ask for things that they knew were out of our control. It got me to thinking about how much time we spend on these "What if?" scenarios. What if this happens? What if that happens? And a lot of times those what-ifs are followed by a negative, and by things that we can't control.

Which essentially paralyzes the process of moving forward, or puts us in the corner crying for the rest of the night.

So the challenge for next week is simply this:

Although you need to have the "What if," conversation, spend more time on the what-ifs that you can control.

And if you're willing to have the, "What if things don't go well?" conversation, be willing to have the, "What if things do go well?" conversation, too. Because if you know that this thing ends in a celebration, you're going to put more into it.

Just gotta take care of each other. Alright, people, that's all I've got. We're all in this thing together. Have a great week, everybody… Go Crickets!

Self-Reflection Questions for the Leader:

- How often do you find yourself worrying about factors outside your control? How can you shift your focus to what you can influence and impact?
- How can adopting a "What if things do go well?" mentality affect your team's morale and productivity? Can you think of a situation when having a positive outlook led to a better outcome than expected?

"What If?" Scenario Planning Session

- Activity Overview: Facilitate a scenario planning session at which staff members explore both challenging and positive "what if?" scenarios and develop strategies for each. Encourage a focus on the potential for celebration and success to motivate effort and optimism.

Momentum

As students flood back into classrooms, bringing with them the energy and excitement of a new academic year, teachers ride a similar wave of adrenaline. This initial burst is a powerful force, driving educators through long days and new challenges. However, as the weeks progress towards the winter break, the initial energy wanes and the reality of the long haul ahead becomes apparent. School leaders play a pivotal role during this transition, guiding their staff through this period with strategic support and empathy. Recognizing the signs of fatigue and burnout is the first step; addressing them proactively is the next.

Creating a supportive environment where teachers feel valued and understood is essential. Leaders can implement regular check-ins, not just about academic progress but also as a barometer for teacher well-being. Providing access to professional development focused on self-care and classroom management can offer teachers fresh strategies to reinvigorate their teaching and personal resilience. Moreover, fostering a culture in which staff members feel comfortable sharing their struggles and successes builds a strong, supportive community. Encouraging peer mentorship and collaboration can also lighten individual loads, making the daunting more doable.

In addition to emotional and professional support, practical measures can make a significant difference. Adjusting timelines, reducing non-essential tasks, and ensuring ample prep time can help people manage workloads.

Celebrating small wins and milestones can boost morale, reminding teachers of their impact beyond the daily grind. Organizing staff appreciation events or simple gestures of gratitude can further uplift spirits. Ultimately, by actively listening, adapting to needs, and fostering a culture of care, school leaders can navigate their teams through the challenging months, ensuring a positive, productive environment for teachers and students. This holistic approach not only sustains momentum toward the winter break but also reinforces the foundation for a resilient and engaged teaching community. Welcome to Season Two…

My 3

**Alright, everybody, Saturday morning,
Fall Creek, Wisconsin, one minute walk to work,
and here's what I'm thinking about today...**

So I'm lying in bed this morning thinking about the impact of the number three on my life, and I guess I tend to do things in threes. I guess I tend to do things in threes. When I speak to groups, I always tend to come back to three concepts. In some cases we are talking about being intentional about the work, opening doors to those around us, and building staff capacity. At other times I am talking to groups about telling stories at schools through finding your audience, building your brand, and celebrating kids. Another example is creating a culture of storytellers through recognizing the great work of the adults, acknowledging that great work, and extending it to those who don't get to see it every day. Even our school board has three norms. The first is that we operate under the idea that the answer is always *we*. The second is that we always keep our dirty laundry in-house, and the third is that we never pass up the opportunity to say something great about our schools.

So I guess it always kind of comes back to the number three. I don't know if that's because third grade was the best two years of my life or what, but at the same time, we do an activity with our staff called "My 3," and in that activity, we ask them to write down what three things would have to happen throughout the course of the day to make the day successful for them. And I think that really helps provide focus on what they value, even though we know that there are hoops that must be jumped through during the course of any given day. And for me it was, do I help people smile? Do I help them think? And do I help them feel? If I can help people smile, think, and feel, then the day is going to be successful for me, but it's also hopefully providing value for somebody outside of my space.

▶▶ So the leadership challenge for next week is simply this:

What three things would have to happen throughout the course of the day to make the day successful for you? Same thing for your staff. Same thing with your students. Write these things down, have a visual not only so they can see them, but also so when you go into their space, you can help provide feedback for something that they value. Everybody's A to B is different. If you don't value their A, there's no chance you can help them get to their B.

**Just gotta take care of each other. Alright, people, that's all I've got. We're all in this thing together. Have a great week, everybody...
Go Crickets!**

Self-Reflection Questions for the Leader:

- What are my top three priorities for today, and how do they align with the needs and values of staff and students?

- How well am I understanding and supporting the individual goals and values of staff and students?
- What can I do to better align my leadership practices with the diverse needs and aspirations within my school community?

Daily Success Planning: "Visualize Success"

- Activity Overview: Have staff and students create visual representations of three things that would make their day successful, fostering a culture of understanding and support for individual goals.

LEADERSHIP CHALLENGE WEEK 12:

Unscheduled Moments

**Alright, everybody, Saturday morning,
Fall Creek, Wisconsin, one minute walk to work,
and here's what I'm thinking about today...**

Before the school year started, I got a chance to go back to Pulaski, Wisconsin, and help them kick off their school year. I actually started my teaching career in Pulaski in 1997, teaching second grade. It's actually the second time that I've been back to Pulaski to help them kick off their year. The first time was in 2016, and that day hit hard because there was a new teacher in the audience that day named Colin, who was actually a second grader in my class eighteen years before that day. It was really interesting. The conversations with Colin were really interesting because the things that he remembered about second grade were not the same things that I remembered about second grade. He remembered all the unscheduled moments that happened in second grade. He remembered conversations that I don't remember us having. He remembered throwing a football at recess. He remembered my reaction to his classmates' behavior.

And I remembered the work. I remember every bulletin board that we put up. I remember building a four-by-eight space shuttle, so these kids had a fancy area to read in. I remember the paper mache cornucopia activity that was an absolute disaster. We're talking about high-level second grade curriculum here, people. I had no idea what I was doing.

I kept thinking to myself, I wish I could remember the unscheduled moments that he remembered, because the unscheduled moments that he remembered brought him so much joy. The way that he talked about it was just incredible.

So, the leadership challenge for next week is simply this:

Be present in the unscheduled moment, because the unscheduled moment is not only what they remember, but also what brings them a tremendous amount of joy. And that's the story that gets told over and over again. We deserve that, too. Paper mache, cornucopias. I bet they're still pulling the paper mache out of the carpet twenty-five years later, man.

Just gotta take care of each other. Alright, people, that's all I've got. We're all in this thing together. Have a great week, everybody... Go Crickets!

Self-Reflection Questions for the Leader:

- How can I be more present and attentive during unscheduled, spontaneous moments in my school?
- What steps can I take to create an environment in which staff and students feel valued in every interaction, scheduled or not?

Unscheduled Joy Activity: "Moments of Joy"

- Activity Overview: Create opportunities for spontaneous joy in the school day, such as surprise coffee breaks or impromptu game sessions, emphasizing the value of being present in the moment.

Original Thank You

**Alright, everybody, Saturday morning,
Fall Creek, Wisconsin, one minute walk to work,
and here's what I'm thinking about today...**

So, we're a couple weeks into the school year, which means we're a couple weeks removed from the "Welcome back to school" gatherings that people hosted. I love "Welcome back to school" gatherings, just seeing people reconnect. It's incredible, actually. But there's something special about bringing a group of people together for the first time. But, there's a script to it, too. We get people in and then we welcome them and we introduce the new people, and then we say thank you for all the work that's been done to make sure that the school year is ready to go. I guess I'm thinking about it a couple weeks out because I'm wondering, "When does the second thank you take place? Then the third thank you, and the fourth thank you throughout the course of the year?" Because the further that we get from the original thank you, the more that the original thank you feels like it was part of a script to start the year.

If the next thank you is during the nationally recognized appreciation week for that particular area, the original thank you means very little, which I have been absolutely guilty of in the past. We spent a lot of time talking about how we want kids to come back to school excited for the next day. How often are we having the same conversation about the adults taking care of the kids? Because it's less about coffee and donuts and tacos and pizza, and more about conversations and connections–well, pizza's different because… pizza. But if you can help people to laugh, to smile, and to think and to feel on a daily basis, they're going to come back feeling happier. But, they're also going to make other people feel happier too.

 ### So, the leadership challenge for next week is simply this:

People remember things that break the script. So break the script on gratitude and thanks. One of the things that pulled me out of a rut this week was simply saying thank you to people for things that I had seen them do or had heard they had done from a colleague. It not only broke the script for them; it forced me to recognize the great things that were happening around us.

Just gotta take care of each other. Alright, people, that's all I've got. We're all in this thing together. Have a great week, everybody… Go Crickets!

Self-Reflection Questions for the Leader:

- How am I expressing gratitude in unique and meaningful ways to all staff members?
- What innovative approaches can I use to show appreciation that might be unexpected but impactful?

Gratitude Break Script: "Gratitude in Action"

- Activity Overview: Encourage staff members to write thank you notes or verbally express gratitude for specific actions or qualities they appreciate in their colleagues, breaking the routine and fostering a positive environment.

LEADERSHIP CHALLENGE WEEK 14:

Be. Clear.

**Alright, everybody, Saturday morning,
Fall Creek, Wisconsin, one minute walk to work,
and here's what I'm thinking about today...**

I t's a little dreary today, but the weather in Wisconsin has actually been pretty good over the course of the last couple of weeks, which is great because we have a lot of kids who ride their bikes to school every day. And our kids are so excited about school that they'll often miss the bike rack and dump their bike at the door and just run into school because they can't wait to get invested in the learning process, which has caused a little congestion at one of our doors.

I was a little frustrated with it and was talking to one of our teachers about it. She said that the day before they had actually talked to three kids about making sure that their bikes got in the rack, and we went out to the bike rack and, of course, what three bikes are in the bike rack the next day but those three that they talked to.

I think from a leadership lens there are often times that I hide behind the idea that people should just know, kids should just know, adults should just know. They should just know without actually setting a clear expectation of what it looks like. You know, John Wooden may be the best basketball coach of all time–if he's not, he's certainly in the conversation. He would always spend his first practice of the year with these high school and college All Americans teaching these guys how to tie their shoes. He wanted to make sure that they didn't get blisters, but he also wanted to make sure that they knew there was a clear expectation about how things were supposed to be done.

So, the leadership challenge for next week is simply this:

If we truly believe that people are doing the best they know how, then we must be willing to help with the "how." And if I get frustrated with someone for not meeting an expectation that they don't know about, then the only person I can be frustrated with in that scenario is me. I really think people are trying to do the best they can all the time. We just have to trust them.

Just gotta take care of each other. Alright, people, that's all I've got. We're all in this thing together. Have a great week, everybody… Go Crickets!

Self-Reflection Questions for the Leader:

- How clear am I in communicating expectations and providing the necessary support to meet them?
- What steps can I take to ensure that I am not holding others to unspoken standards?

Leadership Activity: "The Expectation Reflection"

- Activity Overview: Facilitate a group discussion during which participants share experiences of unmet expectations due to a lack of knowledge. Use these stories to create a shared document of explicit expectations and strategies for effective communication.

Build Capacity

**Alright, everybody, Saturday morning,
Fall Creek, Wisconsin, one minute walk to work,
and here's what I'm thinking about today...**

I find it interesting how sights, smells, and times of year often bring up memories that just slap us right in the face and this time of year always brings up a memory from my third year of teaching, which was literally twenty years ago. I remember my principal coming into my classroom after school one day and telling me that there was a parent of one of our students who had decided that this wasn't the right space for them and that they were going to move the student to the classroom across the hall. I remember being absolutely devastated by that because I kept thinking to myself, what have I done? I mean, I can't believe I didn't make a connection with this kid, but what it also did was make me very hesitant to share any of the stuff that was happening in our class.

I was just really self conscious that I wasn't nearly as good as the person across the hallway and I think this happens a lot in school. I think a lot of the best ideas that happen in school often die before they exit the classroom walls because we're afraid of what our colleagues are going to say about that idea. They don't think it's as good of an idea as we think it is and they think, "Don't do that because if you do that then I'm going to have to do that and I don't think I'm ready to do that. So don't do that."

 ## So, the leadership challenge for next week is simply this:

Building collective efficacy in a school often starts with making sure that people feel value in their own space. We've talked about the idea that we want to, as leaders, recognize the great work that's happening, acknowledge the great work to the person that's doing it, and then extend the conversation to somebody who wasn't there so they also know the great work is happening. But how do we move to an environment where that's not leader dependent, it's just what we do? Because when we all feel value in our space, we're more willing to share and that becomes a spot where we can build momentum.

Just gotta take care of each other. Alright, people, that's all I've got. We're all in this thing together. Have a great week, everybody... Go Crickets!

Self-Reflection Questions for the Leader:

- How am I fostering an environment in which recognition and value are inherent in our school culture?
- How am I acknowledging and utilizing the unique strengths of each staff member?

Collective Efficacy Workshop: "Value Circles"

- Activity Overview: Conduct a workshop during which teachers form small groups to discuss and recognize each other's contributions. Each group will then share their acknowledgments with another group, fostering a culture of recognition that is not dependent on leadership.

LEADERSHIP CHALLENGE WEEK 16:

Peak and End

**Alright, everybody, Saturday morning,
Fall Creek, Wisconsin, one minute walk to work,
and here's what I'm thinking about today...**

I got a letter in the mail this weekend. It was addressed to Superintendent Joe Sanfelippo. What I've come to learn in this profession is that when you get a handwritten letter addressed in that manner, it's not always a great letter. A couple of weeks ago, when I was doing one of these walks, I had mentioned my fourth grade teacher, Mrs. Gephardt, and that I didn't remember everything that she taught me, but I did remember her smile at the door every day. My mom had seen that video as well, and she reached out to Mrs. Gephardt, so when I looked at the letter and I saw Mrs. Gephardt's name as the return address, I just kind of sat there and stared at it for a second.

I was hoping that it wasn't a report card. I read the letter and it was very nice. She didn't mention all the trouble that I got into, or that I pretended to read during silent reading or all the candy that I stashed in my desk, that she clearly knew that I had in there. She

60

just said, "I'm proud of you." She was happy that I decided to get into this wonderful profession of education. It came at the perfect time because I know my energy level hasn't been nearly as high as it was when we started this whole process, but when you get a letter that is signed: Your Fourth Grade Teacher, Pier Elementary School, class of '84-'85, you realize the impact that teachers have on kids.

So, the leadership challenge for next week is simply this:

Chip and Dan Heath wrote a great book called *The Power of Moments* (2017). In it, they talk about the idea that people remember two things about events: the peak and the end. Our people were fully invested in the peak of this crisis. But how do we help them stay invested in the end? Because if we can stay invested in the peak *and* the end, then that's what kids and families are going to talk about for years to come.

Just gotta take care of each other. Alright, people, that's all I've got. We're all in this thing together. Have a great week, everybody... Go Crickets!

Self-Reflection Questions for the Leader:

- How can I ensure that both the peak and end moments of our initiatives are impactful and memorable?
- What strategies can I implement to maintain staff engagement and enthusiasm through the conclusion of projects or crises?

Peak and End Focus Group: "Memorable Milestones"

- Activity Overview: Staff members collaborate to create and celebrate significant milestones in school projects or initiatives.
- Heath, C., & Heath, D. (2017). The power of moments: why certain experiences have extraordinary impact.

 LEADERSHIP CHALLENGE WEEK 17:

Model Breaks

**Alright, everybody, Saturday morning,
Fall Creek, Wisconsin, one minute walk to work,
and here's what I'm thinking about today...**

Yesterday, I saw an online graphic that had pictures of Bob Ross, LeVar Burton, Mr. Rogers, and Steve Irwin. The caption read: "Some of our best teachers taught virtually." Though all these men have had an impact on my life at some point, they also had full production crews. Their shows were thirty minutes long, all right? Our people are doing this all day, every day, and man, they are tired. Thankfully, our staff has a full week break next week. We told them that we want them to take a step back from the day-to-day operation of school and really invest in the people who they care about the most. Because a lot of times we think that the people that they care about the most often give them the most latitude during school, and they shouldn't have to.

I think saying that is one thing. But I think as leaders, we need to take an active role in allowing people to break away from school. At times, in an effort to inform, I tend to overwhelm, which impacts whether people can actually break away from school. You know, I'll send an email out just so they have the information when they come back. Or I'll send a text message, and then at the bottom I'll write: "Just FYI." Like writing "Just FYI" fixes the whole thing. It may take something off my mind, but it puts it directly on theirs. Our job is to do exactly the opposite of that.

So, the leadership challenge for next week is simply this:

If you want to appreciate staff during a break, model what it means to actually take a break. We told our staff yesterday that they're not going to hear from us until next weekend at the earliest, so don't check your email. I think we just need to take a collective break as a group. And you may ask, "Well, then Joe, why are you walking to school on a Saturday?" People, I got granola stashed in my office because if I keep it at home, my kids are going to steal it. I'm just going for breakfast.

Just gotta take care of each other. Alright, people, that's all I've got. We're all in this thing together. Have a great week, everybody... Go Crickets!

Self-Reflection Questions for the Leader:

- How effectively am I demonstrating the importance of taking breaks and disconnecting for personal well-being?
- In what ways can I reinforce the message that taking breaks is essential and valued in our school culture?

Embracing Breaks Activity:
"The Unplugged Challenge"

- Activity Overview: Challenge staff members to truly disconnect during a break, with no work communication allowed. Share personal stories of how taking real breaks has rejuvenated your commitment and focus.

Embed Support

**Alright, everybody, Saturday morning,
Fall Creek, Wisconsin, one minute walk to work,
and here's what I'm thinking about today...**

We're in between breaks here and I am continuously amazed at the work that the people in this building do to continue to engage kids in what's going on here, because it is tough and they need a break. And I hope when they get a break, they take a step back and realize the impact that they've had on those around them. And I think one of the things that we try to do as leaders is to support people throughout, but there are times when I feel like I'm reactionary in that support and I only support when they absolutely need it, as opposed to embedding it into a system that they live every single day. When I coached, I would tell kids after a tough game, "Hey, great job tonight. No practice tomorrow." Or when I was a principal, I canceled meetings in the morning so they had more time to plan throughout the course of the day.

And even last week, it was beautiful here. So we told people, "Get out early. Take time, take advantage of the sun, because it's going to get real cold here real quick." And those are all fine gestures, and I think people really appreciate that, but is it embedded into the work they do on a day-to-day basis?

 So, the leadership challenge for next week is simply this:

What are we doing to make sure that we embed support into the system that we provide for our people? Are we giving them an opportunity to have conversations or just get caught up on their PD or not scheduling things that puts them at the edge? Because if we wait to support people until they're at their breaking point, they can never truly be their best.

Just gotta take care of each other. Alright, people, that's all I've got. We're all in this thing together. Have a great week, everybody… Go Crickets!

Self-Reflection Questions for the Leader:

- How am I proactively embedding support mechanisms within our school to prevent staff from reaching a breaking point?
- What can I do to create more opportunities for staff to engage in meaningful conversations, professional development, and wellness activities?

Embedded Support Strategy Session: "Supportive Systems Design"

- Activity Overview: Host a collaborative session to design systems and practices that embed support into the school's fabric, ensuring staff members feel valued and understood before reaching a breaking point.

Look Up!

**Alright, everybody, Saturday morning,
Fall Creek, Wisconsin, one minute walk to work,
and here's what I'm thinking about today...**

The last two weeks around here have been pretty tough. Most of the tough stuff is about things we can't control, but I still have a hard time letting that stuff go. So it does impact the way that I walk around school and it hit me this week when I was on the playground, one of our elementary kids just yelled out, "Sanfelippo, look up, watch me!" And he just started running. He just wanted me to watch him run. I'm watching him run and I'm cheering. I'm smiling. And in that moment, all the frustration and the anxiety of the things that I couldn't control just kind of slipped away.

Honestly, the anxiety came back as soon as I got back to my office, but after that I found myself in more places with more kids and more staff members. Doing this helped me be less concerned with things I couldn't control. The tough stuff didn't go away, but my perspective was also much different when I had to deal with it.

Tough things are going to happen. But when we let the tough things that happened yesterday preclude us from seeing the great things that happen today, we get further away from the reason that we love the job and closer to the reason that we don't.

 So, the leadership challenge for next week is simply this:

Look up. If I didn't look up, I would have missed the kid on the playground. I would've missed talking to the fifth-grade teachers about how great it is to have kids back in school. I would've missed watching a high school teacher beam with pride as she watched her kids run a coffee shop. I would've missed walking into a kindergarten class and having a kid rub my head and tell me that it was OK because his grandma's kind of bald, too. I would've missed standing outside of a four-year-old kindergarten class and watching our high school kids walk out smiling, and laughing, and joking because they just met the four-year-olds that they get a chance to teach some science lessons to in the next couple weeks. I would've missed all of it. So look up. Chase the smiles. Because when you do, you're going to find theirs, but you're going to find yours, too.

Just gotta take care of each other. Alright, people, that's all I've got. We're all in this thing together. Have a great week, everybody... Go Crickets!

Self-Reflection Questions for the Leader:

- How often am I taking the time to "look up" and notice the small, joyful moments in my school?

- What can I do to ensure that I am present and engaged, appreciating the little things that make my school unique and vibrant?

Mindfulness Walk: "Chase the Smiles"

- Activity Overview: Organize a walk around the school or local area during which participants are encouraged to "look up" and notice the positive around them. Encourage sharing of the smiles and joys noticed during the walk.

LEADERSHIP CHALLENGE WEEK 20:
Every Interaction Matters

**Alright, everybody, Saturday morning,
Fall Creek, Wisconsin, one minute walk to work,
and here's what I'm thinking about today...**

I don't know if you've seen this aging challenge on social media, but it got me to thinking about things years ago, and so before I was a principal and after I was a teacher, I was a counselor in Ashwaubenon, Wisconsin, and so, in that role, I used to go into classrooms regularly.

And when I went into classrooms, we'd do an icebreaker activity to kind of start the session. And one of the icebreaker activities that I did was, I told kids we were going on this picnic, and they had to bring something to the picnic, but they had to figure out that the thing that they could bring had to start with the same letter as their first name. So you know, Peter could bring pizza. You know, Sanfelippo could bring soda or whatever. And so, anyway, fast forward ten years later, and I'm back in Ashwaubenon connecting with a former student who actually just graduated with an education degree. Congratulations, Jake.

And, of course, we get in that moment, and we take the selfie, and we post the selfie, and there was a response to the tweet that said, "Are you bringing sandwiches to the picnic?" And I had to look at it for a second, and I'm thinking, "What is he talking about?" But then I realized that it was from the activity. Now, here's the thing about the activity. I did it one time, ten years ago, and that's what the kid remembered. And it got me to thinking: every interaction matters because we never know which one they're going to remember.

So, the leadership challenge for next week is simply this:

Be intentional with every interaction because it could be the one that they talk about ten years later. We work with kids. I gotta be honest. I can make you a promise. You're going to be remembered. The only question is how.

Just gotta take care of each other. Alright, people, that's all I've got. We're all in this thing together. Have a great week, everybody... Go Crickets!

Self-Reflection Questions for the Leader:

- How can I ensure that my every interaction, no matter how brief, is positive, meaningful, and leaves a lasting impact?
- What steps can I take to model this approach for staff, ensuring that they, too, understand the importance of every interaction?

Interaction Impact Activity: "The Memory Maker"

- Activity Overview: Encourage staff members to share stories of interactions that had a lasting impact on them, reinforcing the power of intentional engagement. How does this shape the way you interact with others?

LEADERSHIP CHALLENGE WEEK 21:

What You Do
with the Time

**Alright, everybody, Saturday morning,
Fall Creek, Wisconsin, one minute walk to work,
and here's what I'm thinking about today...**

So this week I was in Texas working with school principals in a district of about seventy schools, which is exciting and humbling, by the way.

And every time I'm working with a group, I always do two things. One of the two things is to take people through the *recognize, acknowledge,* and *extend* model, because I want them to see both the impact of the model and the amount of time that it actually takes for the process.

So this week was really cool because we were in the room and a principal stood up and acknowledged some of the great work that one of her teachers was doing in front of the entire district. And it was great.

And she sat down and a different principal from the other side of the room stood up and told a story about the same teacher who she had worked with years before in a different district, in a different state, actually, which was really cool.

So of course, we messaged the teacher, let the teacher know that she was being talked about, and we get a message back from the teacher that says, "This made my year." It was a text message.

Think about how many of those you've already sent today. The whole process from start to finish took 90 seconds: 30 seconds to recognize the greatness of a colleague, 30 seconds to acknowledge it, and 30 seconds to extend the conversation to somebody who wasn't there. 90 seconds.

So, the leadership challenge for next week is simply this:

Recognizing, acknowledging, and extending is not more work. It's the right work done more. And when you look at it like that, you're more likely to realize the impact and maybe make someone's year. It's not about the time; it's what you do with the time. Every time.

Just gotta take care of each other. Alright, people, that's all I've got. We're all in this thing together. Have a great week, everybody... Go Crickets!

Self-Reflection Questions for the Leader:

- How am I maximizing the use of my time to make the greatest impact in my leadership role?
- What strategies can I implement to encourage efficient and effective use of time among our staff?

Impactful Recognition Activity:
"The Recognition Relay"

- Activity Overview: Start a relay of recognition where a staff member acknowledges another's work, who then passes the recognition on to someone else, illustrating the ripple effect of positive feedback.

Assume Good Intentions

**Alright, everybody, Saturday morning,
Fall Creek, Wisconsin, one minute walk to work,
and here's what I'm thinking about today...**

Yesterday I was walking down the first-grade hallway, and I saw this kid at the bubbler, and he had his water bottle at the back of the bubbler. So all the water was coming down to fill the water bottle, and the water was going everywhere. It was overflowing. It was creating this huge mess. So I start walking towards the bubbler faster because I felt as though I needed to redirect the kid. I've got to tell him he's making a huge mess, talk about the waste of water and everything like that. And as I get close to the bubbler, he looks up at me. He goes, "I can't stop it. Can you help me?" Of course, I can help you. So I help him get the top on.

And he looked at me. He said, "It's my birthday today."

"Oh, that's fantastic, buddy," I said, "How old are you?"

He goes, "Six years old." And then he goes right into, "Hey, are you a gamer?"

I said, "No. I'm not a gamer."

He goes, "I'm a gamer. I play Minecraft. I used to be a Noob, then I was a Pro, and I'm a Hacker."

Fantastic. "How long have you been playing Minecraft?"

He goes, "Sixty years."

I said, "Wait, how long?"

He goes, "Yeah, sixty years."

The best looking 66-year-old I've ever seen in my life. It was one of the best conversations I had all week, and not at all what I thought it was going to be as I approached that bubbler.

▶▶ So, the leadership challenge for next week is simply this:

If you're going to assume something about somebody, assume the positive. I would much rather assume the positive and be wrong, because it impacts the way that I walk into those interactions. And we all know every interaction matters, because every interaction could be the one that they talk about for the rest of their lives. I hope this kid has the best 66th birthday party ever today.

**Just gotta take care of each other. Alright, people, that's all I've got. We're all in this thing together. Have a great week, everybody...
Go Crickets!**

Self-Reflection Questions for the Leader:

- How am I practicing the assumption of good intentions in my interactions with staff and students?
- What steps can I take to foster a culture of positivity and trust within the school?

Positive Assumption Exercise: "The Best Interpretation"

- Activity Overview: Engage in role-playing scenarios where staff must interact based on positive assumptions about one another, highlighting the impact of positivity on school culture.

LEADERSHIP CHALLENGE WEEK 23:

Connect the Network

**Alright, everybody, Saturday morning,
Fall Creek, Wisconsin, one minute walk to work,
and here's what I'm thinking about today...**

Our people just got back from the Thanksgiving holiday. What a great opportunity to connect with their networks and really kind of step away. So I'm thinking about the actual term "Thanksgiving" because the giving part matters, right? Has anyone ever told you that it's the thought that counts? Though I understand the premise, I don't think it's the thought that counts. I think it is the action on the thought that counts. Thinking about something doesn't put it into action. The thought may count, but the action counts more as it leads to something more. The holiday is not called "Thanksthinking." Let's understand that.

So the leadership challenge for next week is simply this:

Everybody has a network. All your staff members have a network. Our job is to try to connect those networks. So reach out to the networks of people on your staff. It doesn't matter if it's their spouse or if it's their kids, or if it's their aunts or uncles, or if it's their parents. Making a call to the parents of a staff member just to make sure that the parents know that that staff member is incredible is an unbelievable opportunity. Don't ever forget that everybody is somebody's kid. It doesn't matter if they are 4, 14, 24, or 44. Everybody is somebody's kid.

Just gotta take care of each other. Alright, people, that's all I've got. We're all in this thing together. Have a great week, everybody... Go Crickets!

Self-Reflection Questions for the Leader:

- What opportunities exist to leverage these networks for mutual benefit, both for the staff and the wider school community?
- Reflect on the impact of acknowledging the personal backgrounds of your staff. How does this influence your leadership style?

Connecting Networks Activity:
"The Network Web"

- Activity Overview: Create a visual web of connections by having staff members list their personal and professional networks on sticky notes and then linking these networks on a large wall or board. Discuss ways to engage these networks to support and enrich the school community.

LEADERSHIP CHALLENGE WEEK 24:

Break the Script

**Alright, everybody, Saturday morning,
Fall Creek, Wisconsin, one minute walk to work,
and here's what I'm thinking about today...**

Our daughter, Allie goes to gymnastics four days a week, and it's about a twenty-five minute drive from home. I try to take her every opportunity that I can. So essentially I've driven that route about a thousand times at this point. And we get to the door and I tell her that I love her, and she gets out and I'll sit in the parking lot. And there are days that I can't even remember how I got there. I just got there. It was just a routine. I think we do this in schools a lot. We start our day the same way, we end our day the same way. We connect with the same people throughout the course of the day. And then the days turn into weeks, and the weeks turn into months. And the next thing you know, it's twenty years later and they're giving you a watch for twenty years of service to the organization.

Routines are great, but the moments that we remember often fall outside of those routines; they break the script. Even video conferencing. Video conferencing a year ago was kind of exciting. And a year later it's just turned into a routine. And even in that routine, it becomes monotonous. Doesn't it? You're logging onto the video conference and someone says, "How's everyone doing?" How's everyone doing??? We're teaching during a pandemic. That's how everyone's doing.

So the leadership challenge for next week is simply this:

Break the script. Walk down a different hallway. Connect with different people throughout the course of the day. Start your day and end your day with different routines outside of what you normally do. And if you're in that video conference, instead of starting it with, "How's everyone doing?" start by asking someone to tell a story about a colleague who's doing great things for kids. And then extend that conversation to that colleague to make sure that they know that they're being talked about. And if their colleague is actually in the room with you, then extend the conversation to somebody in their world so they know that they're being talked about.

The moments don't have to be about these big events. Doesn't have to be about prom, graduation, twenty years of service. More often than not, these moments are the ones that break the script: connecting with someone, telling them that you care about them or that you see them, that you hear them, that you value what they bring to the organization. Creating value doesn't happen by accident. And spoiler alert: nobody's wearing that watch. But they will remember the conversation that broke the script.

Just gotta take care of each other. Alright, people, that's all I've got. We're all in this thing together. Have a great week, everybody... Go Crickets!

Self-Reflection Questions for the Leader:

- In what ways am I challenging my usual routines to foster new connections and experiences within my school community?
- How can I encourage and model the importance of breaking the script to create meaningful, value-driven moments?

Break the Script Challenge: "Day of Difference"

- Activity Overview: Challenge staff members to "break the script" with a day dedicated to new interactions, pathways, and routines, reflecting on the impact of these changes at day's end.

Recognize the Struggle

Alright, everybody, Saturday morning, Fall Creek, Wisconsin, one minute walk to work, and here's what I'm thinking about today...

It's the end of the first semester, which means there's a tremendous amount of anxiety around students, parents, teachers, everybody with grades and report cards, everything that goes along with it, and it got me thinking about when I was teaching. I remember my first year teaching, I had this young man in class that just simply wouldn't listen to anything that I had to say. Anything. Wouldn't do his work, distracting other kids, the whole thing. And I remember calling my mom and telling her about it, and I was telling her, "He won't listen. He won't do anything that I have to say." So I go to work the next day and I come home, and there's a message on my answering machine–because I'm that old at this point. And it was my mom, and she said, "I just want to read you something really quickly." She started reading this, saying, "Joe is off task often. Joe distracts his classmates. Joe doesn't work to his full potential." She was reading one of my old report cards, and she said, "You know? You turned out OK. Give the kid a break."

I think oftentimes, we focus so much on the task not getting done, and we don't think about *why* the task didn't get done. Everybody's going through something. It doesn't matter if they're four, 14, 24, or 44. I think oftentimes, relationship building is less about our actions and more about our reactions to where people are coming from.

So, the leadership challenge for next week is simply this:

Just recognize the struggle that people are going through and either help them with that struggle or connect them to somebody who can.

Just gotta take care of each other. Alright, people, that's all I've got. We're all in this thing together. Have a great week, everybody... Go Crickets!

Self-Reflection Questions for the Leader:

- Can you recall a period in your life when you faced difficulties and how others' understanding or lack thereof affected you? How does this reflection impact your approach to students or colleagues who may be struggling?
- How can understanding the underlying reasons for a student's or colleague's behavior change your response and potentially improve the situation? How might this approach foster a more supportive and inclusive school environment?

Struggle Support Network: "Connecting Circles"

- Activity Overview: Host a session where staff identify personal and professional struggles and collaboratively brainstorm support networks and resources available within and outside the school.

Recognize, Acknowledge, Extend

Alright, everybody, Saturday morning, Fall Creek, Wisconsin, one minute walk to work, and here's what I'm thinking about today...

A couple of summers ago we were playing baseball with our three year-old nephew, Patrick, and as we're getting ready to pitch him the ball, he's going to hit, my son Aiden says to him, "Patrick, can you hit the ball?"

And Patrick drops his bat, looks at Aiden as though he's got nine heads and says, "I can do anything. I can do anything."

So he hits the ball, he starts running around the bases. People are just jacked up and cheering for him. "Way To go, Patrick. You can do it, Patrick."

He steps on home plate, puts his hands in the air and says, "Yay me."

"Yay Me." He was so proud of what he had accomplished. As educators, I think at some point we stopped being proud of the work and we started defending the work. And I think there's a distinct difference between being proud of the work and defending the work. We use words like "just" and "only." I'm *just* a teacher. I'm *only*... When we devalue our work, it gives people outside of our space licensed to do the same.

 So, the leadership challenge for next week is simply this:

First of all, recognize something incredible that's happening in your space. Then acknowledge it to that person, that it's incredible, and then extend the conversation to somebody who wasn't there to let them know it was incredible. People aren't going to change the way *they* talk about schools until *we* start changing the way that we talk about schools. Patrick said, "Yay me," as he simply ran around some bases. I just think people changing the lives of kids should be able to say the same.

Just gotta take care of each other. Alright, people, that's all I've got. We're all in this thing together. Have a great week, everybody... Go Crickets!

Self-Reflection Questions for the Leader:

- What strategies can I implement to more widely share and celebrate these successes?
- How regularly do I recognize and acknowledge the achievements of our staff and extend these recognitions to others?

Incredible Acknowledgment Activity: "The Acknowledgment Tree"

- Activity Overview: Create a visual "tree" where leaves represent acknowledgments of incredible things happening in the school, encouraging a culture of recognition and positive talk about education.

Renewal

You wake up, and it's dark. You go home from work and it's dark. The third season of the school year is about helping others find purpose when the holidays are gone and the breaks are few and far between. Providing joy for others often starts with making sure we can see it for ourselves.

As the winter break fades and the long stretch before spring break begins, school leaders face the critical task of re-energizing their staff. The post-holiday period can often leave teachers feeling drained, grappling with the challenge of reigniting their own enthusiasm and that of their students. Recognizing and addressing this fatigue is paramount. Leaders can infuse new energy by introducing innovative teaching methods or technology, providing fresh avenues for educators to engage their students. Offering professional development opportunities focused on self-care and stress management can also empower teachers, enabling them to manage their well-being effectively alongside their professional responsibilities.

Moreover, fostering a culture of appreciation and support plays a vital role in uplifting staff morale. Simple gestures, such as personal notes of thanks, public recognition of hard work, or small tokens of appreciation, can significantly boost spirits. Encouraging peer support and collaboration can also strengthen the sense of community within the school. Leaders should ensure they're accessible, offering an open door for teachers to share concerns, successes, and suggestions. By actively listening and responding to staff needs, school leaders can cultivate a nurturing environment that not only acknowledges the hard work and dedication of educators but also renews their passion for teaching as they navigate the demanding months leading up to spring break. Trust for what we do as leaders is built in the times that surprise us. How we respond when everyone is at a tough spot in the year will be how they respond to the group they serve. Our behavior will set the tone, and the more consistent we are in that behavior, the more conversations we will invite, which in turn, leads to fewer scenarios that surprise us. Welcome to Season Three...

We're Just Part of the Story

**Alright, everybody, Saturday morning,
Fall Creek, Wisconsin, one minute walk to work,
and here's what I'm thinking about today...**

L ast night, one of our kids scored their 1,000th point in a high school basketball game. Congratulations, Joey. Really good accomplishment. Everybody in the crowd knew when he only needed to score one more basket to get to 1,000, so every time he touched the ball people were just going nuts, and they're just waiting, and encouraging and everything. Then he scores, and the crowd goes bananas!

It was awesome. Earlier this week, I was talking to one of my high school friends, and he was coaching his daughter's fifth grade girls basketball team. One of the little girls on that team hadn't scored all year. In the last game of the year, they're doing everything they can to get this little girl a basket. Every time she touched the ball, the crowd is just ready for the score. The ball never goes in the basket for her.

As I'm talking to him, I can feel the emotion on the other side of the phone, because all he wanted for her was to be successful and just have that feeling. It got me to thinking: here are two kids on both sides of the scoring spectrum. Joey's put the ball in the basket hundreds of times here, and this little girl hasn't done it once. Yet at the same time, when they had the ball, the encouragement from those around them was the same. They just want them to be successful. That's all they wanted.

▶▶ So, the leadership challenge for next week is simply this:

We need to recognize where people are at and support where they want to go, but we also have to understand that it's their journey and not ours. We're just part of the story.

Just gotta take care of each other. Alright, people, that's all I've got. We're all in this thing together. Have a great week, everybody... Go Crickets!

Self-Reflection Questions for the Leader:

- How well do I understand and support the individual journeys and goals of my staff and students?
- In what ways can you better facilitate and respect the personal and professional growth paths of those you lead?

Journey Support Activity:
"My Journey, Our Support"

- Activity Overview: Facilitate discussions during which staff members share their personal journeys and aspirations, focusing on how colleagues can support each other's paths without imposing their own directions.

Joy in the Mess

**Alright, everybody, Saturday morning,
Fall Creek, Wisconsin, one minute walk to work,
and here's what I'm thinking about today...**

Kids are back from break right now and they're talking about what they did over break. That got me to thinking about years ago, when my son, Kael, said all he wanted for Christmas was a set of bongo drums. That's it. So of course, being the parents we are, we get him a set of bongo drums. He opens up bongo drums on Christmas morning and he's so excited, laughing, smiling, having a great time for about twenty minutes until his older brother opened his present, which was a brand new iPhone.

Then that smile turned into a smirk, that smirk turned into a scowl, and then he started to tell us all the reasons that he should get the phone before his older brother. The joy he had in the bongos was lost when he started to think about what he didn't have: the iPhone.

So, the leadership challenge for next week is simply this:

Find joy and purpose in the present. Think about how often we look across the hallway or on the other side of the building or in a different district or on social media and we see things happening there and we think that it must be better there. Time that we spend doing that takes away from the time we could be finding joy in what we currently have. That this building is incredible and of course we have messes, but one of the things that I respect the most about the people in this building is that they find joy in the mess.

They help kids to smile and to laugh and to think and to feel, and they do the same thing for their colleagues. And that's made much easier when you're present in the moment and you wake up every morning knowing that your work has value.

Just gotta take care of each other. Alright, people, that's all I've got. We're all in this thing together. Have a great week, everybody... Go Crickets!

Self-Reflection Questions for the Leader:

- How am I finding and appreciating joy in the complexities and challenges of my daily work?
- What can I do to encourage my team to embrace the present and find joy and purpose in their current roles?

Present Joy and Purpose: "Find Joy in the Mess"

- Activity Overview: Organize a "Joy Hunt" within the school, where staff and students look for and share moments of joy and purpose amidst the everyday chaos and challenges.

Recognize Purpose

**Alright, everybody, Saturday morning,
Fall Creek, Wisconsin, one minute walk to work,
and here's what I'm thinking about today...**

2020 was absolutely awful for a number of people, and as 2020 came to a close, I think there were a lot of people who were really excited about what 2021 was going to bring. And then one week into 2021, and people start to question whether things are going to change at all. Reminds me of when I was a kid and our teacher used to roll in that big cart, with that huge tube television on it, into the classroom, and people got really, really excited until you realized it was the human growth and development video and then nobody wanted to be there anymore.

2020 was a mess, but I have to believe that within that mess, you found some joy. And guess what? 2021 is going to be messy, too, but part of our jobs as leaders is to help people recognize their purpose when they don't realize the impact that they're having on those around them.

So the leadership challenge for next week is simply this:

When people don't recognize their purpose in the mess, then the mess becomes the only thing that they can see, and our job is to help them recognize their purpose. We talked about doing that activity, that "My 3" activity, where you have staff members write down what three things would have to happen throughout the course of the day to make that day successful. When they write those down, it helps them recognize their purpose. When you know what they are, you can either help them or connect them to somebody who can–especially in the mess

Just gotta take care of each other. Alright, people, that's all I've got. We're all in this thing together. Have a great week, everybody... Go Crickets!

Self-Reflection Questions for the Leader:

- How am I facilitating the recognition of individual purposes among staff, especially in challenging situations?
- What strategies can I use to ensure that staff members feel aligned with their core values and goals amidst daily challenges?

Purpose in the Mess Activity: "Purpose Mapping"

- Activity Overview: Facilitate a group activity where staff map out their personal and professional purposes, especially in challenging times, to maintain focus and motivation.

You are the Reason

**Alright, everybody, Saturday morning,
February in Wisconsin, one minute walk to work,
and here's what I'm thinking about today...**

Fall Creek, Wisconsin is really interesting because you look outside and it's fantastic. Then you walk outside and it's nine degrees and you're thinking, "What are we really doing here?" It's a tough time of year for staff, too, because you're in that stretch where there's not a lot of breaks. People are getting sick, the adults are getting sick, which means that there's more substitute teachers in the building. The kids are getting sick–well,most of the kids; there's the one kid who never gets sick. You know this kid. Never sick, never sick. He's there every single day. You want to say to this kid some days, "You look kind of tough. You could probably use some rest," because you need a break, too.

That was me. I was this kid. I was there every day. I was there early in the morning. I was there late at night. I was there at your desk. I was asking the questions, I was in all your stuff, I was there all the time, but I could genuinely tell you at the age of 11 whether or not you wanted to have me in your classroom or not. I think what we have to understand is the way that we talk to these kids has a profound impact on how they interact with us when they're there every single day. I can tell you that I don't know if I missed a day of school in fourth grade, but it had more to do with the fact that I knew Mrs. Gebhardt *wanted* to have me in class everyday or she *made me believe* that she wanted to have me in class everyday. I don't know which one it was, but I certainly remember her smile at the door every day,

▶▶ So, the leadership challenge for next week is simply this:

This is a tough time of year for our people, and it's our job to make sure that they know their value at this time of year. You know, a teacher can get frustrated that the kid is there every single day. But if they know that they are the reason that the kid is there every single day, then they treat that kid differently because they know that they are the reason that the kid is there every single day.

Just gotta take care of each other. Alright, people, that's all I've got. We're all in this thing together. Have a great week, everybody... Go Crickets!

Self-Reflection Questions for the Leader:

- How am I acknowledging and reinforcing the impact my staff has on students, especially during challenging times?
- What am I currently doing to ensure that every staff member feels like a vital part of our students' success?

Value Recognition Activity: "The Reason They Come"

- Activity Overview: Engage in discussions or reflections on the importance of recognizing the impact teachers have on why students show up every day, fostering a sense of value and purpose.

Stop Comparing

**Alright, everybody, Saturday morning,
Fall Creek, Wisconsin, one minute walk to work,
and here's what I'm thinking about today...**

I was speaking to a group this week–actually in Wisconsin–and the night before, I went out to dinner with some friends and after dinner we were walking out of the restaurant and then there was another group walking into the restaurant. We stopped and talked a little bit and a woman came over to me and said, "Joe, I really like those one minute walk to work talks that you do," and I said, "Well, thank you so much. I appreciate that."

Then she said, "You're much taller on Twitter." I laughed and my friends laughed. They had heard it before.

It got me thinking about social media and how we use it. What we need to understand about social media is that we see everybody's best on social media. When we see everybody's best, it often hinders us from sharing our own story because we're afraid that it doesn't have as much value as the stuff that we see online. What you must understand is that movements are started when a collective story is shared. I say that we're all in this thing together, and I do it intentionally because everybody's story helps contribute to changing the way that people talk about school.

▶▶ So, the leadership challenge for next week is simply this:

Stop comparing yourself to what you see online and start using the ideas that you see there to amplify the voices of those around you a little bit more. The stuff that you're doing is just as good as the stuff that you see online–and you're probably taller, too.

Just gotta take care of each other. Alright, people, that's all I've got. We're all in this thing together. Have a great week, everybody... Go Crickets!

Self-Reflection Questions for the Leader:

- How do I balance inspiration from external sources with valuing and amplifying the unique contributions of my team?
- What can I do to help staff focus on their strengths rather than comparing themselves to others?

Social Media Reality Check:
"The Authenticity Project"

- Activity Overview: Encourage staff to share real stories of success and challenge, contrasting the often idealized portrayals seen online, to celebrate authentic experiences and achievements.

LEADERSHIP CHALLENGE WEEK 32:
Listen to Understand

Alright, everybody, Saturday morning, Fall Creek, Wisconsin, one minute walk to work, and here's what I'm thinking about today...

Yesterday I was having a conversation with our food service director, Val–who's a phenomenal leader by the way. And we were talking about high expectations and helping others grow and developing leadership capacity and everything that goes along with it. And got me to thinking about my first couple of years as a principal. I feel like I was much more of a help desk than I was a leader because people would call and they'd ask for help and I'd just run to their classroom right away. And instead of helping them through the problem, I just fixed it because I knew how I wanted it done and it was just easier for me to do it that way.

What ended up happening was people who wanted things done would call and ask for help. And the people who actually wanted help stopped calling because they knew I was just going to come down and do it the way that I wanted to do it anyway. And what I had to understand was that *high expectations* doesn't automatically mean *my expectations*. Everybody's voice matters.

▶▷ So, the leadership challenge for next week is simply this:

Helping and doing are not the same thing. When we expect ourselves in those we lead, we deny them the opportunity to develop their unique leadership voice. We also hinder the group moving forward, because we're only coming at it from one perspective. The ideas of people in this building are a lot better than anything I got. I just have to be willing to listen.

Just gotta take care of each other. Alright, people, that's all I've got. We're all in this thing together. Have a great week, everybody... Go Crickets!

Self-Reflection Questions for the Leader:

- How can I improve my active listening skills to better understand and empower my staff?
- What steps can I take to ensure that I am not just hearing, but truly understanding and valuing the perspectives of others?

Leadership Voice Workshop: "Voice Amplification"

- Activity Overview: Conduct a workshop aimed at developing and expressing individual leadership voices within the school, emphasizing listening and inclusivity.

The Next

**Alright, everybody, Saturday morning,
Fall Creek, Wisconsin, one minute walk to work,
and here's what I'm thinking about today...**

I t's been really cold here the last few days, which means I need to get out of that garage and into that school as quickly as I possibly can. Mostly because I don't want to tear up and then have those tears freeze to my face, which is actually something that happens here. But the problem is I think I've been taking on that same mentality when I've been at school, when I'm trying to get to the next thing and to the next thing and to the next thing. And if I'm always trying to get to the next thing, I never get a chance to really kind of be present and engaged with the people in the space. I think part of it is because that I'm a list guy. I love lists, things that I need to do, people I need to connect with, and I like lists because when I get done with something on the list, I can cross it off and feel like I've accomplished something.

I mean there are times that I'll actually add things to the list that I've already done just so I can cross them off, because I should get credit for that stuff. Honestly. The problem with the list is that it's turned into a routine. So I get to work in the morning and I turn my computer on and I check my email and I review the list, and then I sign some forms and then I go out and talk to people, which is what I really want to do. By the time I go out and talk to people, I'm already in the wrong mindset because everything that I read on the email has now just been added to the list and I feel overwhelmed.

▶▶ So, the leadership challenge for next week is simply this:

Think about the first ten things that you do when you get to school every day and then ask how many of those things bring you joy? And all we want to do is try to move those things up on the list just a little bit. Everything on the list needs to be done. But all of them are made much easier if you're in the right mindset to do them. And if there's nothing on the list that brings you joy, you're going to want to add that. And maybe don't cross that off for a little bit. It's just really hard to connect with people if you're not in the right mindset to do so.

Just gotta take care of each other. Alright, people, that's all I've got. We're all in this thing together. Have a great week, everybody... Go Crickets!

Self-Reflection Questions for the Leader:

- What daily activities bring me joy and how can I prioritize them to enhance my effectiveness as a leader?
- What steps can I take to encourage staff to prioritize activities that bring them fulfillment?

Joy Prioritization Activity: "The Joy List"

- Activity Overview: Have staff members list and share the first ten things they do at school, highlighting and discussing how to prioritize joy-bringing activities.

We Get What We Model

**Alright, everybody, Saturday morning,
Fall Creek, Wisconsin, one minute walk to work,
and here's what I'm thinking about today…**

Yesterday was "Snow Fest" here, so our high school kids got a chance to interact in different capacities with our teachers and it was a really cool day. It got me to thinking about, when I was a principal here, one of the things we used to do on Friday's is to have some kids come down and play Plinko and they could win awards such as, lunch with a teacher, extra recess for their class or be the assistant principal for the day.

I remember once a Kindergarten student won the "assistant principal for a day" thing and we're walking down the hallway. Because he's the assistant principal for the day we're stopping at classrooms and as we stop at the classroom, he'd walk into the classroom and shake the hands of the teachers and say, "If you need anything today, just let me know." Which in and of itself is adorable. As we're walking down the hallway, at some point I must have picked up some trash and thrown it away because a few months later, he was in the building with his dad for "Donuts with Dad" and as he's walking down the hallway with his dad, he starts picking up some trash and throwing it away and his dad said, "You know, what are you doing buddy?"

He said, "Dad, this is what we do here to help out."

It got me thinking that, you know, we often get what we model. You can get a pretty good indication of a building by walking down the hallway and seeing how the adults interact with each other.

⏩ So, the leadership challenge for next week is simply this:

Be mindful of your adult interactions because young eyes are always watching and they always have a story. When kids go home from school, they may not tell their parents what they did at school, but they will most certainly tell their parents what they saw at school. We just want to make sure it's the right story.

Just gotta take care of each other. Alright, people, that's all I've got. We're all in this thing together. Have a great week, everybody... Go Crickets!

Self-Reflection Questions for the Leader:

- How do my interactions with colleagues and students reflect the values I want to instill in our school community?
- In what ways can I improve my behavior or communication to serve as a better role model for students?

Adult Interaction Awareness: "Eyes of the Young"

- Activity Overview: Conduct role-play exercises to simulate the perspective of students observing adult interactions, promoting mindfulness of behavior and its impact on school culture.

Every Conversation

**Alright, everybody, Saturday morning,
Fall Creek, Wisconsin, one minute walk to work,
and here's what I'm thinking about today...**

S o a couple years ago, I got a chance to go back to the elementary school that I attended as a kid. And it was summer, so there was no one around. So I got a chance to just kind of walk through the hallways and reminisce a little bit. And the interesting thing to me were the feelings that came up as I walked down different hallways in this school. You walk down the hallway towards the gym and the playground, feel really good. Walk down the hallway towards the principal's office and I'm immediately taken back to the day that I called my principal, Mr. Bright, "not-so-bright" in front of everyone and got sent to the principal's office. In that moment, I honestly felt like I was walking a little bit faster to get past the principal's office to get to a different hallway. Because I just wanted to be in a place that I felt a little bit more comfortable.

And I think I find myself fighting that here a lot because there are certain hallways and times of the day that are really convenient for me to get to, which means that the people in those hallways and at that time of day, get more of me than anyone else. And the conversations that we have are literally about nothing, but they happen. And it's great for the people in that conversation, but it doesn't do anything to build credibility or relationships with anybody else in the organization.

⏩ So, the leadership challenge for next week is simply this:

Think about how you spend your day, who you spend your day with, where you spend your day. How many conversations about nothing are you having with people in your organization? Because I'll tell you this, the conversations about nothing have a profound impact on your credibility when you have to have a conversation about something. And the more conversations about nothing that you have, the easier it is for everyone in that space to have a conversation about something.

Just gotta take care of each other. Alright, people, that's all I've got. We're all in this thing together. Have a great week, everybody... Go Crickets!

Self-Reflection Questions for the Leader:

- How am I ensuring that my everyday interactions, even those about "nothing," are building trust and credibility?
- What strategies can I employ to make my casual conversations more impactful and meaningful?

Credibility through Connection:
"Nothing Conversations"

- Activity Overview: Initiate a challenge whereby staff are encouraged to have meaningful "conversations about nothing" with colleagues, building trust and credibility within the community.

3 Stories

**Alright, everybody, Saturday morning,
Fall Creek, Wisconsin, one minute walk to work,
and here's what I'm thinking about today...**

I recently got three messages from teachers telling me there were things that I had to see. One was in a classroom, one was in a hallway, and one was some video reflections of our high school kids after they had just finished teaching a science lesson to our four-year-olds. The teachers were so proud of the work that these kids were doing. I was so thankful that they were willing to talk about this work because I think too often, we do these great things in classrooms that we're proud of, but we don't talk about them because we're afraid of what the reaction is going to be.

I find that really interesting because in our personal lives, I don't think that we feel that way. Because I can tell you what you're proud of right now. Go to your photos app, I'll tell you exactly what you're proud of. You're proud of kids, pet, house, car, hunting, fishing, cabin, boat. It's all on your phone. You'll tell stories about that stuff all day.

I think in schools, it's just the opposite. How often do you go next door to a colleague and have a conversation about a schedule change or have a conversation about something that you're struggling with? Versus how often do you go next door to a colleague and tell them that you just taught a lesson that you're really proud of? We go and go and do and do, and I think a lot of times we're in classrooms and you don't think that the work that you do is that big a deal because you keep just doing the work. When in fact, what you're really doing is changing the lives of kids. That's a big deal.

⏩ So, the leadership challenge for next week is simply this:

Tell three stories to three colleagues about the great things that are happening in your space. In this building, that's 360 stories, 360 stories to build momentum and pride around the work that we do. That's also 360 opportunities for those stories to be told beyond the walls of our school. That's how we build momentum.

Just gotta take care of each other. Alright, people, that's all I've got. We're all in this thing together. Have a great week, everybody... Go Crickets!

Self-Reflection Questions for the Leader:

- How and with whom am I actively sharing positive stories from our school?
- What strategies can I use to encourage a culture of sharing and celebrating each other's successes?

Storytelling Momentum: "360 Stories"

- Activity Overview: Launch a storytelling initiative in which each staff member shares three positive stories about their work or their colleagues, aiming to collect and share a large number of uplifting narratives.

Find Joy in Others

**Alright, everybody, Saturday morning,
Fall Creek, Wisconsin, one minute walk to work,
and here's what I'm thinking about today...**

This is the time of year that people start to feel isolated, and it's harder to find joy in the work when you feel isolated in the work. I think if you ask educators anywhere why they do this work, almost all of them will tell you why they do the work. But knowing *why* you do the work and actually *seeing it* on a regular basis can sometimes be two different things, and that's when we need each other. Jim Valvano was a coach at NC State, and they won an NCAA tournament. When you mention Jim Valvano's name, everybody goes to the "Don't Give Up, Don't Ever Give Up" speech that he gave at the ESPYS, which is brilliant. But the clip that I love from Jim Valvano is after they won the title at the buzzer, everybody's going crazy, and you just see him running around the court just looking for someone to hug. He just wanted to share in the joy with his people.

▶▶ So, the leadership challenge for next week is simply this:

Moments are special because of the people in the moment. We become isolated, it starts to feel lonely and even depressing if you feel like you're the only person going through it. And that's when we need our colleagues to help out. You need to go next door and have some deep philosophical conversation about how you got here. It's just about being in the same space so everyone feels like they're seen and they're heard. And if you can help each other laugh and smile and think and feel on a regular basis, everyone comes back to school happier the next day. It's easier to find joy in the work when you're helping other people find theirs.

Just gotta take care of each other. Alright, people, that's all I've got. We're all in this thing together. Have a great week, everybody... Go Crickets!

Self-Reflection Questions for the Leader:

- How am I finding joy in the successes and happiness of my colleagues and students?
- What can I do to create a more collaborative and supportive environment in which everyone can find joy in each other's achievements?

Colleague Support Day: "Shared Spaces"

- Activity Overview: Designate a day for staff members to share spaces and activities intentionally, focusing on creating and sharing moments of laughter, thoughts, and feelings to enhance community well-being.

Permission to Lead

Alright, everybody, Saturday morning, Fall Creek, Wisconsin, one minute walk to work, and here's what I'm thinking about today...

I got a call from a high school teacher and he was really excited to tell me a story about something that happened in his class. And so he was telling me that he was getting prepared for class and had to pop out of the room right before the bell rang. So when he walked into the room, the bell had already sounded. As he walked into the room, one of our high school seniors was already at the whiteboard doing the review of the material that they had learned the day before. And there are so many things that I want to unpack here, but before I even get into any of those, I just wish you could have heard the pride and the joy in his voice, man. He was so excited. He was so proud of her. He was so proud of his class. It was just awesome.

But logistically let's think about this. We had a kid who was confident enough in both the content and the environment to lead, even though she wasn't technically in charge of that environment. We had a teacher who was willing and encouraging to let her lead. And we had a group of peers that allowed it to happen. That's what we want.

⏩ So, the leadership challenge for next week is simply this:

Are we creating an environment where those we lead will lead without asking permission to lead? We spend so much time talking about how we want to create the leaders of tomorrow, then we don't let them lead until they leave. If the people that you lead know that you'll support the decision that they make, they're much more likely to make that decision and step out of their role to lead.

Just gotta take care of each other. Alright, people, that's all I've got. We're all in this thing together. Have a great week, everybody... Go Crickets!

Self-Reflection Questions for the Leader:

- How am I cultivating an environment that encourages and supports leadership initiatives from the team without them seeking permission?
- What actions can I take to demonstrate my trust in the team's decision-making and leadership abilities?

Leadership Without Permission: "The Lead the Way"

- Activity Overview: Host a forum where staff can share ideas and initiatives they've led or want to lead, encouraging a culture in which leadership is taken without waiting for permission to lead. Provide opportunities for staff to lead the way on projects they are passionate about and find time to allow them to share that passion and process with the staff.

The Power of a Positive Conversation

Alright, everybody, Saturday morning, Fall Creek, Wisconsin, one minute walk to work, and here's what I'm thinking about today...

Earlier this week I was in the office, and I got a call from my sophomore son, Kael, and he gets on the phone. I said, "Hey, buddy, what's up?"

He says, "Hey, Dad, just calling to check in."

I said, "Oh great. Thanks so much, man. What do you need?"

He responded, "No, Dad. I'm just calling to check in and see how you're doing." And so we go back and forth with conversation and at some point in the conversation I stop him and I'm thinking, "Kael, what did you do?" I was expecting him to tell me something that he did to his brother or to his sister or to the house or maybe he sold the dogs online or something like that. I don't know. He said that he had spent the morning calling his teachers just to check on them, to see that they were OK.

He said, "Dad, they all called us, to make sure that we were doing all right. I wanted to make sure that somebody called them, checked on them, and made sure they were doing OK, too." He said, "Dad, it felt really good."

So in that moment I couldn't decide whether I was more proud of my kid or the impact that our people had on my kid. I just knew that it felt really good.

▶▷ So, the leadership challenge for next week is simply this:

Don't ever underestimate the power of a positive conversation. The more that we lean into those we serve, the better chance we have for those we serve to lean into others. Do you know what I mean? In a week that we honor teachers, the most honorable thing about teachers is the connection that they make with kids, even when they don't get the immediate gratification of that connection. And teachers, the way they see you; my goodness, thank you. All I can say is thank you.

Just gotta take care of each other. Alright, people, that's all I've got. We're all in this thing together. Have a great week, everybody... Go Crickets!

Self-Reflection Questions for the Leader:

- How am I using positive conversations to inspire and motivate staff and students?
- In what ways can I create more opportunities for meaningful and positive interactions within the school?

Positive Conversation Week: "Lean In with Kindness"

- Activity Overview: Dedicate a week to having positive conversations, focusing on leaning into service and support for others, and reflecting on the impact of these interactions.

Culmination

With the end of the year now in sight, state testing approaching, graduation requirements and ceremonies coming up, and next year's budgeting process beginning, school leaders are tasked with an essential, yet challenging, role: to serve as the anchor for their staff during the times when many students are looking at what is next. Either graduation, the next grade level, or, in most cases, an extended break. Keeping them engaged comes with anxiety and stress, where the well-being of the adults, who are taking care of the kids, must take precedence. Leaders can alleviate some of this pressure by ensuring clear communication about expectations and available resources. Offering workshops or sessions on stress management techniques and time management can equip staff with tools to navigate their responsibilities more effectively.

In these final months, it's crucial for leaders to foster an environment of support and understanding. Regular check-ins with staff to gauge morale and address concerns can make a significant difference. Leaders should prioritize recognizing the hard work and achievements of their team, perhaps through informal gatherings or personal acknowledgments. Such gestures of appreciation can boost morale and foster a positive school culture. Ultimately, by focusing on creating a supportive atmosphere that prioritizes the well-being of all staff members, leaders not only enhance their team's capacity to manage end-of-year challenges, but also lay the groundwork for a resilient and motivated workforce ready to inspire and educate the leaders of tomorrow. Welcome to Season Four...

LEADERSHIP CHALLENGE WEEK 40:

We Don't Get to Choose

**Alright, everybody, Saturday morning,
Fall Creek, Wisconsin, one minute walk to work,
and here's what I'm thinking about today...**

I was in the lunchroom this week and a fifth grader called out from his table, "Sanfelippo, what's the joke?"

I'm thinking, "What are you talking about?" I walked over to his table and said, "What are you talking about?"

He responds, "The joke. What's the joke of the day? You used to do the joke of the day."

And I still had no idea what he was talking about, so I said, "Who was your teacher when I used to do the joke of the day?" And he told me who his teacher was, and it was his kindergarten teacher. I'm thinking, "Man, that was five years ago." I couldn't remember.

The next morning I walked into his classroom and I opened the door and I screamed, "Kids, kids, kids, kids, don't trust the stairs… They're always up to something."

As soon as I said it, I looked over at him and you could see his eyes wrinkle up a little bit. You knew he was smiling behind the mask. And he laughed and he said, "That's it. It's the joke of the day." And the kids in his class exploded and another student yelled, "Oh yeah, the joke of the day."

I have no idea how many jokes I did or how often I did it. But in that moment, as soon as they heard the joke, it brought back a memory and a smile and an eye roll for some.

⏩ So, the leadership challenge for next week is simply this:

Be intentional with every interaction because we don't get to choose which one they'll remember. We can only give them as many opportunities as possible to smile and feel valued because when they do, they'll see more good in the day. It doesn't matter if they're 4, 14, 24, or 44.

Just gotta take care of each other. Alright, people, that's all I've got. We're all in this thing together. Have a great week, everybody... Go Crickets!

Self-Reflection Questions for the Leader:

- The Impact of Small Gestures: Reflect on a time when a seemingly small gesture or action you took had a lasting impact on someone else. What was the gesture, and how did it come to have significance? This question encourages teachers to think about the lasting effects of their daily interactions with students and colleagues.

- Memorable Moments: Consider the interactions you have with your students or colleagues. Which ones do you think they'll remember? Why? This question prompts teachers to reflect on the quality and content of their daily interactions and to consider how they can create positive, memorable moments.

Intentional Interactions: "The Ripple Effect"

- Activity Overview: In the "Ripple Effect" activity, teachers reflect on meaningful past interactions and choose a positive quality to embody, symbolized by writing on a pebble and observing its ripples in water to visualize the impact of their actions. This interactive exercise underscores the importance of intentional interactions within the school community, highlighting how even small gestures can create significant, widespread positive effects.

Opportunity vs. Obligation

**Alright, everybody, Saturday morning,
Fall Creek, Wisconsin, one minute walk to work,
and here's what I'm thinking about today...**

Sometimes I need to be reminded of the impact of every interaction, because I think there are times that I take those interactions for granted or I'm not fully present and engaged in the moment for those interactions because I have something else going on in my mind.

Thursday was a perfect example of that because I was in the lunchroom, but I wasn't really paying attention to anything and the first grade kids came walking around and one of them just latched themselves onto my leg. And I looked down, I said, "Hey, bud, what's up?"

And he said, "How come you're not so excited to see me?"

And I said, "Well, I'm excited to see you."

And he said, "Well, you didn't say anything."

Then he took off and I honestly couldn't figure out why he said it that way until I realized that when he comes in in the morning, I say to him, "I'm so excited to see you today." So when I didn't lead with that in the lunchroom, he's thinking, "Hey, old man, what's up?" I was in the lunchroom, but I wasn't fully present and engaged in the lunchroom.

⏩ So, the leadership challenge for next week is simply this:

Every interaction matters, but more importantly, every interaction is an opportunity. We've talked about the idea that every interaction matters because every interaction could be the one that they talk about for the rest of their lives. And I don't love that, but when I acknowledge that it's real, I look at that interaction as less of an obligation and more of an opportunity. And sometimes I just need a first grade kid to remind me.

Just gotta take care of each other. Alright, people, that's all I've got. We're all in this thing together. Have a great week, everybody... Go Crickets!

Self-Reflection Questions for the Leader:

- How am I viewing each interaction as an opportunity to positively influence my school community?
- What changes can I make to transform obligatory interactions into opportunities for growth and connection?

Opportunity in Interaction:
"The Opportunity Walk"

- Activity Overview: Invite staff to take a walk around the school, engaging in spontaneous interactions with students and colleagues, viewing each as an opportunity to make a positive impact. Be sure to include staff members who don't regularly find themselves in those spaces (business office, human resources, buildings and maintenance).

LEADERSHIP CHALLENGE WEEK 42:

Be in the Moment

**Alright, everybody, Saturday morning,
Fall Creek, Wisconsin, one minute walk to work,
and here's what I'm thinking about today...**

I t's hiring season, and teacher appreciation week is right around the corner, so we think about these two situations and how we're creating value in moments for people in these places. We think about it in two capacities. One is, how do we make sure that they know we want them to come here and, two, how do we make sure that they know that we want them to stay? When it comes to making sure that they know we want them to come here we'll do all kinds of stuff, like going offsite to offer a position to somebody, bringing kids in to offer a position, bringing former teachers in to offer a position, doing the press conference, taking a picture of the family; all that stuff.

More importantly, how are we making sure that they know that we want them to stay? That comes with every interaction that you have with your group. I'm going over now to write notes in cards for our staff members for teacher appreciation week, and I'm at my best when I can open those cards and get to a specific situation that I've seen them in. I'm at my worst when I can't remember the last time I had a conversation with them.

 ## So, the leadership challenge for next week is simply this:

Creating moments means being in the moment. I had a professor in our doctoral program who used to say to us, "The greatest gift of service that you can give to another human being is, for the time that you're with them, they are the center of your universe." I think, as leaders, if we keep that in the front of our mind, we're going to be better for it.

Just gotta take care of each other. Alright, people, that's all I've got. We're all in this thing together. Have a great week, everybody... Go Crickets!

Self-Reflection Questions for the Leader:

- How present am I during interactions with staff and students, and what can I do to improve this?
- How do I practice being fully present and attentive in my interactions with staff and students?

Center of the Universe Activity: "The Gift of Attention"

- Activity Overview: Practice giving undivided attention to others in conversations, making them feel like they are the center of the universe, thereby enhancing mutual respect and understanding.

LEADERSHIP CHALLENGE WEEK 43:

Appreciate Who They Are

**Alright, everybody, Saturday morning,
Fall Creek, Wisconsin, one minute walk to work,
and here's what I'm thinking about today...**

Next week is Teacher Appreciation Week, so administrators across the country are putting together their plans for how they're going to celebrate incredible staff members: the gift cards, the personal days, the notes, food, and snacks, and anything they can do to acknowledge the great work that happens in the building. One of the things that I think we need to be really clear about is that the stuff is great, but the words and actions behind the stuff mean just as much, if not more. Earlier in my administrative career, I remember having a conversation with an incredible teacher. She was fantastic. Parents loved her. Kids loved her. Colleagues loved her. She was a very well-respected, incredible leader.

I asked if she ever thought about becoming a principal, and she laughed and shrugged it off. We just went on to a different topic and didn't talk about it again. But a couple of days later, I was walking

146

past her classroom, and she asked me to come in. I could tell she was frustrated, and I sat down, and she said that she'd been thinking a lot about the conversation that we had had. She said all she ever wanted to do was be the best teacher she possibly could be, and in that moment I made her feel like she was supposed to be something else.

 So the leadership challenge for next week is simply this:

When you value people in the building, make sure you value *who they are*, not *who you think they should be*. We spend so much time telling people they're not just teachers. Make sure your actions reflect those words. Mine didn't. I'm glad she said something because hundreds of kids are better because she was their teacher.

Just gotta take care of each other. Alright, people, that's all I've got. We're all in this thing together. Have a great week, everybody... Go Crickets!

Self-Reflection Questions for the Leader:

- How am I ensuring that I appreciate and value staff for who they are, rather than who I think they should be?
- What steps can I take to better understand and acknowledge the unique contributions of each individual in my school?

Valuing Individuality: "The Authenticity Circle"

- Activity Overview: Conduct a circle discussion where staff members share experiences of feeling valued for who they are, not who others think they should be, fostering an environment of acceptance and authenticity. Keep notes on the conversations for later reference and/or to make connections to other staff members who may have similar interests or desired paths.

LEADERSHIP CHALLENGE WEEK 44:
Positive Intention

**Alright, everybody, Saturday morning,
Fall Creek, Wisconsin, one minute walk to work,
and here's what I'm thinking about today...**

In the past month, I have visited Texas and Florida. One of the really interesting things about being in Texas and Florida in the month of February is how people walk into buildings versus how they walk into buildings in Wisconsin. Because in Texas and Florida, people just walked into buildings, and they were almost smiling. You walk into a building in Wisconsin during the month of February, and all you're trying to do is avoid -10 degrees. Your eyes, you've got tears in your eyes that are frozen already. The wind hurts your face. And all you want to do is get in the building. You're either in a bad mood because of what you just dealt with, or a better mood because you don't have to deal with it anymore.

Either way, you're letting something that you can't control impact something that you can. I mean, we do this with people all the time. Our reaction to someone else's behavior is often the thing that's going to be talked about twenty years from now. We don't have to love that, but we do have to acknowledge that it's real.

▶▶ So, the leadership challenge for next week is simply this:

What if we took the first five interactions to start our day and treated those as though they were going to be the ones that are talked about at the class reunion twenty years from now. Positive intention creates momentum for you, but also for the people with whom you connect. Now, it may mean that you need to get up ten minutes earlier and get some coffee in your system before you see anybody. But starting your day with purpose sets the tone for how you're going to react to things you can't control.

Just gotta take care of each other. Alright, people, that's all I've got. We're all in this thing together. Have a great week, everybody... Go Crickets!

Self-Reflection Questions for the Leader:

- How am I ensuring that my first interactions each day are positive and impactful?
- What can I do to set a tone of positivity and intentionality from the start of each day?

Morning Intention Activity: "The First Five"

- Activity Overview: Encourage staff to treat their first five interactions of the day as potentially life-changing moments, setting intentions to create positive momentum.

 **LEADERSHIP CHALLENGE WEEK 45:**

Favorites

**Alright, everybody, Saturday morning,
Fall Creek, Wisconsin, one minute walk to work,
and here's what I'm thinking about today...**

I got an email this week from someone who attended a keynote that I gave recently, and this person was upset about a story that I told during the keynote. It's a story that I've told literally hundreds of times over the course of the last eight years. This is the first time that I've ever had that reaction to the story. I give this person a ton of credit for their willingness to reach out, because that's a tough email to write. The irony is that earlier that day, I got another email from someone who was at the same keynote, and this person loved the presentation, and this person specifically referenced the story that the first person was upset about. Same story. Same place. Same delivery. Different reaction. The interesting thing for me was how I reacted to the two emails. I replied to the positive email right away, and I said thank you, and I appreciate it. But the negative email, I looked at that thing ten times just trying to figure it out. I replied and I said, thank you, and I appreciate them reaching out, but it honestly had an impact on the rest of my night. I was less present and engaged for the people who I was with because I kept thinking about that email.

▶▶ So, the leadership challenge for next week is simply this:

You're not going to be everyone's favorite. I'm sorry. You're just not. In a classroom, in a school, in a district, on a stage. You're not going to be everyone's favorite. But the more time you think about not being *everyone's favorite*, the less time you have to actually be *someone's favorite*. Anyone who works with kids has the opportunity to be the one who these kids tell their own kids about someday. You may not be everyone's favorite teacher, but I promise you're going to be someone's. And if you come to school every day knowing that, you treat that space a lot differently.

Just gotta take care of each other. Alright, people, that's all I've got. We're all in this thing together. Have a great week, everybody... Go Crickets!

Self-Reflection Questions for the Leader:

- How am I coping with the fact that I might not be everyone's favorite and focusing instead on being impactful?
- What can I do to remind myself and our staff of the unique and positive impact we each have on different individuals?

Someone's Favorite: "The Favorite Moment"

- Activity Overview: Reflect on the idea that while one cannot be everyone's favorite, they can be someone's. Share stories of impactful teacher-student relationships and discuss ways to be that memorable person for someone.

Just Sit

**Alright, everybody, Saturday morning,
Fall Creek, Wisconsin, one minute walk to work,
and here's what I'm thinking about today...**

I was on the playground recently, literally using it as a shortcut to get from one place to the other. And it was recess time, so there were kids everywhere, and I saw one of our younger elementary kids off to the side by herself. So I walk over to make sure that she's OK and leaned in and said, "Hey, you OK?"

She goes, "Yeah, I'm just sitting."

So I asked her if she wanted to play something, and she looks up at me; she goes, "Nope." And then she looks out past the playground, onto the horizon, and she says, "Sometimes I just like to sit."

After getting past a relatively substantial ego blow of being denied an opportunity to play by a six-year-old, I started walking away and thinking, when's the last time I just sat? I left my office doing stuff to go to a place to do more stuff. And while I was going to that place to do more stuff, I was thinking about all the other stuff that I needed to do. It's not just at school. Think about how many times at home you're sitting on the couch thinking about all the stuff that you need to do. Ironically, while scrolling through social media, watching other people do their stuff, making you think you need to do more stuff.

▶▶ So, the leadership challenge for next week is simply this:

I understand that it's a busy time of year, but find me a time that's not. And if this six-year-old can find ten minutes in her day to just sit, I think we can, too. Some of the best ideas happen when we're not thinking about something else. When we just sit. Look out over the horizon. Feel free to add six-year-old Crickets to the greatest philosophers of all time if you want to.

Just gotta take care of each other. Alright, people, that's all I've got. We're all in this thing together. Have a great week, everybody... Go Crickets!

Self-Reflection Questions for the Leader:

- How often do I take time to sit quietly, and what impact does this have on my creativity and problem-solving abilities?
- What can I learn from the simplicity of a child's perspective

in managing my own professional challenges?

Just Sit Reflection: "The Quiet Ten"

- Activity Overview: Dedicate ten minutes of quiet reflection time for staff, encouraging mindfulness and the generation of ideas in stillness, emphasizing the value of pausing amidst busyness.

Keep Going

**Alright, everybody, Saturday morning,
Fall Creek, Wisconsin, one minute walk to work,
and here's what I'm thinking about today...**

I was watching a video this week, and it was a guy talking about Tiger Woods's chip-in on the 16th hole at Augusta in 2005, which is widely regarded as one of the greatest golf shots of all time, and his contention was it never should have happened. If Tiger Woods would have hit the green on his approach, then he wouldn't have flown over the green and had to chip in. And for us, we wouldn't have been able to see one of the greatest shots that ever happened in golf history. So something bad had to happen for something amazing to happen. And if he would have kept his head down and had it impact his next shot, who knows if that chip even comes close? He just had to keep going. Thirteen years ago, I was a principal in a different school district, and there was a different principal position opening in that school district that I was really interested in, and I thought that I'd be a good fit for, and so I

158

applied for it. When I didn't get the job, I was absolutely devastated. Just devastated. But two weeks later, someone called me and said, you should come out to Fall Creek and take a look at the principal position out here. And I did, and it's been the greatest thing that happened to me professionally. I just had to keep going.

▶▶ So, the leadership challenge for next week is simply this:

Keep going. Just keep going. Sometimes, the thing we didn't get leads to something we didn't even know we wanted and becomes the best thing that has ever happened to us.

Just gotta take care of each other. Alright, people, that's all I've got. We're all in this thing together. Have a great week, everybody...
Go Crickets!

Self-Reflection Questions for the Leader:

- How do I maintain my motivation and resilience during challenging times, and how can I model this for my team?
- What lessons have I learned from past disappointments that have led to unexpected successes?

Keep Going Inspiration: "The Resilience Circle"

- Activity Overview: Share stories of resilience and unexpected positive outcomes from challenges faced, inspiring others to keep going despite obstacles. Develop a personal "Resilience Plan" outlining strategies to stay motivated and focused when things don't go your way.

LEADERSHIP CHALLENGE WEEK 48:

Be There

**Alright, everybody, Saturday morning,
Fall Creek, Wisconsin, one minute walk to work,
and here's what I'm thinking about today...**

Our son Aidan graduated from college yesterday. Shout out to UW-Eau Claire for a fantastic commencement ceremony. And then I rushed out here because it was the high school graduating class of 2023; it was their ceremony as well. One thing struck me about the two graduation ceremonies yesterday, and it was how the graduates walked in. I mean, some were a little nervous, excited, but they were all looking into the crowd to find someone who was there to support them. That took me back to every kindergarten concert I've ever been to. These kids walk in, they walk on the stage, and then they immediately look into the crowd to find their people. And their people are out there, and they're waving, and they're standing up, and they're cheering. They're taking pictures and videos. And then there's that moment. There's that moment where they see each other and they smile. And that's as good as it gets for me. And the same thing happened yesterday. They looked into the crowd to find their people, and they smiled. So from one of their first school experiences in a kindergarten concert to walking across the stage at graduation, they all wanted the same thing. They just wanted to make sure that someone was there to support them.

▶▶ So, the leadership challenge for next week is simply this:

Just be there. Not just physically there, but present when you are there. I know it's the end of the year and I know that you're tired, but if you're going to put your energy into something, put it into every conversation. Because the first few weeks and the last few weeks are much more about the connection than they are about the content. So just be there, because it's better when you are.

Just gotta take care of each other. Alright, people, that's all I've got. We're all in this thing together. Have a great week, everybody... Go Crickets!

Self-Reflection Questions for the Leader:

- How can I enhance my presence and attentiveness in interactions with my team?
- What strategies can I employ to ensure I am fully engaged and present, especially during busy times?

Being Present Workshop: "The Presence Practice"

- Activity Overview: Engage in activities like a mindfulness minute at the beginning of a meeting or active listening workshops that emphasize the importance of being fully present in interactions, discussing how presence can enhance connections and the learning environment.

The Power of One Comment

**Alright, everybody, Saturday morning,
Fall Creek, Wisconsin, one minute walk to work,
and here's what I'm thinking about today...**

Yesterday I got a chance to speak to a group of people and afterwards someone came up to me and said, "Has this whole public speaking thing always come naturally to you?" I immediately responded, "No." I remember the first time I ever spoke in front of a group of people was 7th grade and it did not go well. So, in 8th grade when our 8th grade English teacher told us that we were going to have to memorize and recite a poem in front of our entire class, you can imagine that I wasn't all that jacked up to do that activity.

We were supposed to research all these poems and then tell them which poem we were going to do. I think we've established the fact that I wasn't the most academically engaged student of all time, so clearly I didn't do the research, so when it got to my name, I just picked the first one that I saw, which was the Midnight Ride of

Paul Revere. And you would've thought that I punched somebody. Because everybody in the class did one of those snap turn-arounds and had to be thinking, "Are you kidding me?"

Well, I didn't realize that it was the longest poem, so at this point I'm committed to it because my classmates had all known that I committed to it. So I go and I work as hard as I can to try to memorize the poem. I get to the day, and I recite the poem. As soon as I get done, I took this big sigh of relief that it was over. I asked if anyone had any questions. There was this girl in our classroom, she was sitting two rows and two desks back. She raised her hand and said, "I'm really proud of you."

And I remember everything about that day now because of that one comment. Not only did I feel good about it, but I wanted to do it again.

▶▶ So, the leadership challenge for next week is simply this:

Don't ever underestimate the power of a positive comment to somebody. Not only is it going to make them feel good, but it's going to make them want to move forward and get better at whatever they're doing. Building relationships is hard. But it's not more work. It's the right work done more. You just gotta think about it that way.

Just gotta take care of each other. Alright, people, that's all I've got. We're all in this thing together. Have a great week, everybody... Go Crickets!

Self-Reflection Questions for the Leader:

- How often do I offer genuine, positive comments to staff and students, and what impact does it have?
- What can I do to make giving positive feedback a more consistent and meaningful part of my leadership style?

Positive Comment Chain: "The Kindness Chain"

- Activity Overview: Start a chain of positive comments where each person shares something positive with a colleague, who then does the same, demonstrating the power of supportive interactions. When you are finished, remind staff members to follow up with that colleague in a few days to keep the momentum going.

LEADERSHIP CHALLENGE WEEK 50:

Authentic Connection

**Alright, everybody, Saturday morning,
Fall Creek, Wisconsin, one minute walk to work,
and here's what I'm thinking about today...**

It must officially be summer in Wisconsin. Not because kids are out of school or because the weather is getting better, but because I'm being dive bombed by mosquitoes. They are the size of birds, which is awesome. So yesterday was the last day of school in Fall Creek, and one of the things that resonated the most with me yesterday was the connections that people had as they were leaving the building. From kid-to-kid, kid-to-adult, adult-to-adult. All those conversations were really really cool. All the smiles, all the laughter, all the tears, everything that went along with it made me believe that we had a true connection to the people, and I think when it comes down to it, schools will always be less about bricks and mortar and more about connections and stories. And I think we need to have that conversation more and more.

▶▷ So, the leadership challenge for next week is simply this:

Take time to disconnect, but then find a way to reconnect before everybody is required to be here. Technology has made connection the easiest and the hardest thing to do. I think technology has made it easy to connect *to* people, but I think it's made it much harder to connect *with* people. Find a way to connect with people. Go out to lunch, go to a game. Write a note, do something, be authentic, and you're going to be in a much better place. You gotta think about how we're taking care of each other, not only when we're here, but when we're not. That makes us all better.

Just gotta take care of each other. Alright, people, that's all I've got. We're all in this thing together. Have a great week, everybody... Go Crickets!

Self-Reflection Questions for the Leader:

- How can I use technology effectively to maintain connections without losing the personal touch?
- How do I foster authentic connections in a technology-driven environment?

Reconnect Authentically: "The Connection Quest"

- Activity Overview: Challenge staff to find authentic ways to reconnect with each other outside of technology, such as sharing meals or handwritten notes, emphasizing the value of genuine connections.

LEADERSHIP CHALLENGE WEEK 51:

Luck You Create

**Alright, everybody, Saturday morning,
Fall Creek, Wisconsin, one minute walk to work,
and here's what I'm thinking about today...**

The last three weeks around here have been absolutely bananas. We had the end of the school year. We had the state track meet–congratulations to the Division 3 Girls State Champion–we had graduation. You know, the graduation speaker at UW-Eau Claire a few weeks ago was unbelievable. She was talking about how she was abandoned as a child in another country and then adopted by a family in Wisconsin. And the message was awesome, because she was talking about the difference between the luck you were born with and the luck that you create. She had been extremely lucky to be adopted by the family in Wisconsin, but what she did with that luck is what put her on the stage that day. Lucky things happen. Think about "lucky" inventions, such as penicillin and microwaves and x-rays and velcro. All unintentional discoveries. But the impact was what happened after the discovery was made.

▶▶ So, the leadership challenge for next week is simply this:

We are all unbelievably lucky to even be here. I mean, let's think about it. You're probably watching the video for this leadership challenge in a car or on a boat or at a game or by a pool. Think about how lucky we are to have the access that we have. And when we do that, it makes it easier And Velcro people...You didn't have to put it on the shoe, OK? You could have saved me a ton of embarrassment in middle school, let's be honest.

Just gotta take care of each other. Alright, people, that's all I've got. We're all in this thing together. Have a great week, everybody... Go Crickets!

Self-Reflection Questions for the Leader:

- How do I acknowledge and appreciate the good fortune and opportunities in my life, both personally and professionally?
- In what ways can I foster a culture of gratitude and positive outlook in my team?

Gratitude Reflection: "The Gratitude Dive"

- Activity Overview: Reflect on personal and professional blessings, encouraging a shift in outlook that recognizes and appreciates the luck and access we have, fueling motivation and a positive work ethic. Use a gratitude journal or host gratitude gatherings as motivation.

Never Give Up the Opportunity to Say Something Great About Your School

Alright, everybody, Saturday morning, Fall Creek, Wisconsin, one minute walk to work, and here's what I'm thinking about today...

The last few weeks have just been this constant reflection on what's been going on here for thirteen years. The time that we had to chase a kid down this road, actually. Great conversations with colleagues. Tough conversations with colleagues. Walking into a four-year-old kindergarten class, and having all these kids run at me with the biggest smiles and brightest eyes you've ever seen. All the success that happens in this building. During my interview with the board, I asked them what they're looking for in a superintendent. And one of the board members said, "We've got a lot of really great things happening here, but nobody knows about them." And I told them, I'm not going to be the best superintendent that you'll hire, but I'm the loudest person on Earth. So if there are great things happening here, I can promise you that people are going to know about them. During our last meeting with the staff, I told them that great things happened before I got here and great things are going to happen long after I leave. But how lucky was I to make sure that more people knew about how amazing they are? Because everyone should know the impact that they've had on this community.

▶▶ So, the leadership challenge for next week is simply this:

Never give up the opportunity to say something great about your school. Because when that's our mentality, we can change the way people talk about the amazing things that we do. It has been an absolute pleasure. I hope the walks have helped, but, more impor-tantly, I hope the people in this building always feel the way that I feel when I talk about them. Because they are simply the best thing that's ever happened to my family.

Just gotta take care of each other. Alright, people, that's all I've got. We're all in this thing together. Have a great week, everybody… Go Crickets!

Self-Reflection Questions for the Leader:

- How often do I publicly recognize and celebrate the achievements of my school and team?

- What strategies can I use to ensure that the positive aspects of our school are communicated effectively both within and outside the school community?

School Pride Share: "The Pride Process"

- Activity Overview: Create an easy process for staff to share positive stories and achievements about the school, fostering a sense of pride and changing the narrative about the school's impact on families and students without making them feel as though it is one more thing for them to do.

Acknowledgments

The entire Sanfelippo family has sacrificed for this book. The time it took to put their stories out in the public and understanding that success is not built in a straight line. Andrea always encouraged and understood when I was gone to make the videos on Saturdays. Alena and Kael were ok with stories being told. Aidan was invested in the book from the start. He transcribed the walks, categorized the walks, and played a huge role in starting this book. I truly appreciate his willingness to push this project forward.

Jeff Zoul was integral in the development of this book. As the primary editor of the text, he found a way to keep my voice at the forefront while also keeping that voice readable for those who picked up the book. His questions drove my thinking, and his knowledge of both books and school leadership drove the conversations about the seasons. He was fantastic to work with.

Kheila Casas was responsible for the graphic design of the pages you see and the conversations we had led to the cover idea for the book. The time she took to ensure this book was on the right platforms ensured we could get it to readers at the best time possible. She walked me through everything it took to get a book to market, and for that, I am extremely grateful.

Jimmy Casas and I started talking about this book over a year ago. When I told him I wanted to self-publish the book, he could have tapped out because he has his own publishing company. True to who he is, he walked me through every process and was willing to be there every step of the way. I value his friendship more than he probably knows, and I thank him for every conversation we've had in an effort to get this book to readers.

The Fall Creek School Community is the best thing that has ever happened to my family. I truly hope the village, school board, parents, students, and staff all walk a little taller, knowing their story will continue to be told. Go Crickets.

About the Author

Dr. Joe Sanfelippo was a public school educator for twenty-six years. He has taught Kindergarten, 2nd Grade, and 5th Grade. He was an elementary school counselor and school principal before spending the last twelve years of that career as the Superintendent of the Fall Creek School District in Fall Creek, WI. The Fall Creek School District was named an Innovative District in 2016 and 2017 by the International Center for Leadership in Education. Joe holds a BA in Elementary and Early Childhood Education, an MS in Educational Psychology, an MS in

Educational Leadership, and a Ph.D. in Leadership, Learning, and Service.

Joe has authored multiple books including *The Power of Branding: Telling Your School's Story, Principal Professional Development: Leading Learning in the Digital Age, Hacking Leadership: 10 Ways Great Leaders Inspire Learning That Teachers, Students, and Parents Love* and *Lead From Where You Are: Building Intention, Connection, and Direction in our schools.* He was selected as 1 of 117 Future Ready Superintendents in 2014 and 1 of 50 Superintendents as a Personalized Learning Leader by the US Department of Education in 2016. Education Dive named Joe their National Superintendent of the Year in 2019.